NIHILISM AS IT IS

BEING STEPNIAK'S PAMPHLETS
TRANSLATED BY E. L. VOYNICH,
AND FELIX VOLKHOVSKY'S
"CLAIMS OF THE RUSSIAN
LIBERALS" WITH AN INTRO-
DUCTION BY DR. R. SPENCE
WATSON

LONDON : T. FISHER UNWIN
PATERNOSTER SQUARE

NIHILISM AS IT IS

CONTENTS

*

INTRODUCTION.

Many persons who are interested in the Russian question have explained to me how much they have felt the need of some authoritative information upon the true position of the different sections of the party of reform in Russia towards each other and towards the Russian Government, or, in other words, some explanation of what the aims and doctrines of the Russian Revolutionists, whether extremists or moderate men, really are. This book of Stepniak's, to which Felix Volkhovsky has furnished a chapter, and which also contains the full text of the famous letter of the Revolutionary Committee to Alexander III., and ample quotations from a memorandum of the Russian Liberals to Count Loris Melikoff, will supply this long-felt want. It appears opportunely at a time when extraordinary efforts are being made, by concealing the facts and circulating false information, to induce free peoples to share the methods of that darkest of despotisms, and to become accomplices in its tyrannical treatment of those of its subjects who venture to think for themselves on political or religious matters.

There are already standard works from which English-speaking people can learn much about the Russian Revolutionary Party as it strikes writers who, like George Kennan or Edmund Noble, have carefully investigated the facts. But it is always open to the apologists of the Russian Government to say that these gentlemen are outsiders who have only been shown what it was considered desirable for them to see, and that the Russian Revolutionist speaks with one voice to his foreign friend and another to his allies at home.

But, in addition to such invaluable works as I have mentioned, we have also access to the official documents of the Revolutionary Party which have been published, time after time, in the face of the world, and some of which are, as I have already pointed out, given *in extenso* in this publication. Indeed its special value is that it introduces the reader, so to speak, to the inner life of the so-called, and mis-called, Nihilists. Stepniak's chapters are reprints of pamphlets which were written by him in Russian for Russian readers only ; and they show, therefore, how these men converse with each other, and what the doctrines are which they are preaching from the shelter they have found in England. They show also that the fundamental objects of all Russian Revolutionists (however they may call themselves or be called by others) are the same ; that their struggle is for freedom, national and personal ; and they forcibly urge the necessity of laying aside all matters which are not absolutely essential, and of working closely and unitedly together for those fundamental objects which all alike hold dear.

No one can peruse this book with an open and candid mind without coming to the conclusion that the aims and objects of the Russian Revolutionary Party are such as he can cordially sympathise with,

even should he be unable to accept some of the
views held as to the means employed by the more
extreme party in the great revolutionary struggle.
He will not forget that he is reading of a country
where none of the ordinary safeguards of justice—
freedom of speech, liberty of the press, or popular
representation,—exist; but where, on the contrary,
free thought and free speech are criminal; and
where the Government is all-powerful, and uses
its power tyrannically.

I must not speak about the writers themselves.
They have become well known amongst us. They
are members of that little band of Russian exiles
who have nobly handed down the noble traditions
of those great reformers who found refuge on our
shores in bygone days. But their works, and this
work, speak for them. I hope that this book will
be widely read and carefully considered. It puts
the position of the Russian opposition clearly and
simply before the reader, and it replies convincingly
to the wild and ridiculous mis-statements which the
apologists of the Russian Government are constantly
making. It is of much value. Everything must

be valuable which tends to give a clearer view of one of the greatest struggles for progress and freedom which Europe has seen. Wider knowledge can but increase the sympathy of those who, themselves free, understand the grandeur of that struggle, the triumph of which may be delayed, but cannot be ultimately defeated.

ROBERT SPENCE WATSON.

STEPNIAK'S PAMPHLETS.

THE ORIGIN OF THE BOOK.

THE main part of the volume, for which I have to ask the indulgence of the English readers, consists of two pamphlets of mine written originally in Russian and for the Russians, and which I never expected to be known outside the dominions of the Tzar. But certain attacks upon us some time ago gave me the idea that it might be useful to bring them before the general public.

There are two different and independent organisations working nowadays in this country in their different ways to promote the cause of Russian liberty. The one is the well-known Society of Friends of Russian Freedom, founded in 1890 by Dr. Spence Watson, and now having its ramifications all over the country. It is composed entirely of English men and women, and its activity is confined to foreign countries, its object being the winning over of the public opinion of the civilised world to the interests of Russian freedom. The other society is hardly known to the English, though in

Russia it begins to be known, and rather widely. It is the Russian Free Press Fund—a small publishing company, composed of Russians, supported by Russians, and intended exclusively for supplying the subjects of the Tzar with literature tabooed within the boundaries of Russia.

Both societies have achieved, in their different lines, a success we can fairly term unprecedented, which clearly shows that both were timely and have answered to an actual need ; and it is difficult to say which of the two have proved a sorer thorn in the flesh of the Russian Government.

Those who would like to perpetuate the present ignominious *régime* in our country could not remain indifferent to the fact that the public opinion of the civilised world is gradually passing over to the side of their opponents. Still less could they overlook the effects of a direct appeal to the Russian people themselves, and the fermentations resulting from the spread of scores of thousands of our pamphlets and books among the thinking men and women of our country.

Anyhow, both societies have obtained their full share of recognition in the form of calumnies and insinuations on the part of the host of scurrilous ineptities whom alone the Russian Government was able to muster as its champions, both in the Russian and the foreign press.

Their efforts have done us an excellent service in Russia by making our work known in the spheres which it would take us long to reach with our clandestine publications. In this country we are in no need of this sort of trumpeting-up and underhand advertisement, because we can reach openly all those who may be reached. Yet we must not be ungrateful. These gentlemen (and ladies) have surely done the little they could in strengthening our position, by the display of utter shallowness, mendacity, and evident bad faith of their charges.

To utter against Dr. Spence Watson, Mr. Byles, Mr. Allanson Picton, Miss Hesba Stretton, and a score of men and women of the same standing, the accusation of furnishing money for the dynamite outrages in Russia (which, by the way, have not been heard of for I do not know how many years), was proclaiming themselves at the outset calumniators, deserving nothing but contempt and ridicule. All the men and women who took the lead in the pro-Russian movement in England are known to their countrymen for many years, and it is not for an obscure hireling of the Russian police to throw upon them suspicion of participation in dynamite plots.

Our detractors have brains enough to understand that. Thus a mysterious Mr. " Ivanoff," who some time ago made himself conspicuous by a scurrilous

article in the *New Review*, says explicitly that the
flagrant breach of international obligations on the
part of Dr. Spence Watson and the other members
of the society, must be an unconscious one due to the
diabolical machinations of the "nihilists," with whom
they had the imprudence of associating. The same
is the tenor of Mme. Novikoff's complaint. But
the proceedings of the society are public; the hon.
treasurer, into whose hands all the funds converge,
gives, in the *Free Russia*, detailed accounts both of
the receipts and of the expenditure.

Every penny is accounted for, and improper use
of money is materially impossible, machinations
or no machinations. Mme. Novikoff and her
satellites read *Free Russia* and cannot possibly
be ignorant of the existence of these accounts, and
their specific charge cannot possibly be uttered in
good faith. They not merely say what is false, but
they are fully aware that they are doing so.

But these ladies and gentlemen have a second
line of defence—their citadel to which they would
repair after having been ignominiously defeated in
the first encounter.

Granted that the Society of F. R. F. does not give
any material support to the so-called nihilists who
are fighting the Russian autocracy upon the Russian
soil; granted that all insinuations to this effect are
lies and calumnies, still they would say the fact

remains that these nihilists are anarchists of Rava-
chol's type, and it is utterly inconsistent and improper on the part of the English to give moral
support and encouragement to representatives of the
same party which they prosecute on their own soil.

For all those who have taken the trouble of informing themselves upon the real views and attitude
of the Russian revolutionary party these accusations
will appear as despicable as the former one. I, for my
part, do not believe in their sincerity. The Russian
Government and the Russian police—those at least
who are able to read and write—must know full
well by this time what are the real demands of the
so-called Russian nihilists.

But the mass of the English public, absorbed
by their own affairs, cannot have a very accurate
knowledge of what is going on in a foreign country
thousands of miles away. The champions of Russian
autocracy, who have never been overscrupulous, did
not scruple to avail themselves of this ignorance and
try their best to mislead the public opinion upon this
point.

Nothing can be easier than to confound their alle-
gations by quoting a few lines from the authentic
and authoritative documents which may be called
the official exposition of the views and aspirations
of the Russian revolutionary party. We have done
it during the last campaign against us in the place

where these charges have been uttered, and I do not think that those who have compared the attack and the reply will trouble themselves any more with the question. I may say that, without infringing the rules of modesty, there is surely no glory in getting the better of an opponent like Ivanoff.

But I know well that disposing of one Ivanoff does not mean at all ending the controversy. At the first favourable opportunity some new incarnation of Mme. Novikoff will come forward as if nothing had happened, and will repeat the very same exploded charges and calumnies and insinuations.

With the progress of our work here we may fairly anticipate that these attacks will get more virulent and more numerous. It occurred to me, therefore, that it might be good to publish for the use of our friends and well-wishers a sort of reference book which would give in a concise form the materials necessary for establishing beyond doubt or controversy the real nature, aims, and position of the Russian revolutionists. I owe to our opponents the suggestion how best to do it.

To prove that the programme we put forward before the English is only a mask hiding the face of bloodthirsty partisans of universal destruction, Mr. Ivanoff quotes, or rather misquotes, a pamphlet of mine, entitled " What we want, and the beginning of the end," which he declares to be an appeal to the worst instincts of the human race.

Such a challenge would excuse and justify in any case my bringing that little thing of mine to public notice. Besides, it seems to me that nothing could serve better my double purpose, apologetical on one hand and descriptive on the other, than the publication in English of this pamphlet of mine. When somebody comes to accuse you of having treacherously deceived your friend in company with a third person, some member of your own family, the best plan is to open your drawers and hand over to this friend your private correspondence with that third person. That is precisely what I am doing in publishing in English this Russian pamphlet. But it will have, I hope, more than a polemical interest for an intelligent reader. Being written for Russians, and about Russian affairs and parties, it will of necessity be sometimes obscure for the English. But with some attention the reader will be able to get from it a very clear idea of the physiognomy of our party, of its interior divisions, of the questions which come to the front just now, and also of the special attitude of one little body of Russian revolutionists represented by the Russian Free Press Fund, which has been denounced to them with such incautious vehemence.

To the challenged pamphlet I have joined another :

"The Foreign Agitation." It explains to our Russian friends and sympathisers the aims, the character, and possible influence of the Society of F. R. F. It may be of interest for the English on its own account, and it will at the same time serve as a reply to one of the favourite charges of Mme. Novikoff's set : that of our speculating upon the national hostility of the English toward Russia.

To these pamphlets I have added some documentary evidences : the famous Letter of the Revolutionary Committee to the Tzar Alexander III., some extracts from the collective memorandum of the Russian Liberals to Alexander II. (for which I am indebted to the *Century Magazine* and Mr. George Kennan). Felix Volkhovsky kindly contributed to this book a summing up of the official memoranda of our *Zemstvos.* Put together, these unimpeachable and now historical documents will show to the impartial reader that the aspirations of the so-called nihilist are shared by the best and most representative and authoritative spokesmen of the Russian Society.

I hope the volume will be found timely just now, when the anarchist outrages on the Continent have caused so much confusion, misconception, and misapprehension.

WHAT IS WANTED?

WHAT IS WANTED?

AMONG all nations the transition from absolutism to modern representative government has been accompanied by convulsive and painful struggles. But for no people, perhaps, has the struggle been so hard a one as for us Russians.

Entering so late into the combat for our own and the people's rights, we have found ourselves face to face with a government which could employ in its own defence all the modern improvements in the mechanism of state and all the marvels of contemporary technical science, bringing the size, arming, and power of concentration of the army, as also the art of getting out of financial difficulties, to a degree of perfection of which the upholders of former tyrannies could not even dream.

Another result of our coming so late in history is that the Russian opposition, which has to deal with so powerful an enemy, suffers from internal divisions to an extent which was quite unknown to our predecessors in revolutionary work.

We are far from holding the rather widespread opinion that the more unanimity of views and beliefs there be in any party, the nearer is that party to an ideal condition. No one formula can satisfy all the various characters, temperaments, and intellectual types among the whole mass of people who are capable of being fired with a given idea. Moreover, where there is real earnestness for a cause, all these differences must necessarily show themselves even in the manner of formulating general propositions, and especially in matters relating to the application of such propositions in life. Therefore differences of opinion, within certain limits, are a sign of the intensity of a party's life, and work in common only gains by the existence of differentiated, individualised fractions.

Our misfortune is that to these natural differences of our own we add foreign and artificial differences, which are the result of our equivocal position among the peoples of Europe. While Russia as a whole lives in the eighteenth century of European history, and her peasantry, as it were, in the sixteenth—the age of the Reformation—the Russian educated class stand side by side with the same classes in western Europe; indeed, on the whole, it is even more progressive and receptive than they. We pick up in scraps the latest developments of science, and there is no movement of advanced European thought which does not at once reproduce itself among us. Thus the strife of ideas and the differentiation which in other nations have been spread over a whole series of generations, are concentrated with us into one generation, and we suffer undeserved punishment both for being too progressive and for being too much behind the age. Nothing but the widest mutual tolerance could enable us to avoid the practical consequences of so unfortunate a position. But we are not, and never have been, remarkable for tolerance. It is, therefore, not surprising that the Russian opposition presents a kaleidoscope of parties, which, while working, in essentials, for the same cause, have contrived to become so much divided as to have lost all internal cohesion, and in many cases all capacity—even all desire—to understand one another.

The movement of the years 1873 and 1874,[1] from which the present movement started, was by no means the foundationless thing foisted on us from outside which it may appear to superficial observers. It was a native Russian movement, called into existence by dissatisfaction with the so-called emancipation of the peasants—a reform whose insufficiency had at that time become evident, and not to the young generation alone.

[1] The great pilgrimage of thousands of the educated youth of both sexes "among the peasants" as missionaries of Socialism.

This movement was in reality directed against
our political system, for only a new, free state could
successfully take up and solve the agrarian question.
But the young generation could not formulate its
real desires, and the educated class could not understand the young generation. The young extremists
were left to depend upon their own powers, and this
fact condemned the movement beforehand to complete and fruitless destruction.

The real movement began five years later, when
two-thirds of its supporters had perished, and when
the strength of the first impulse was spent.

Since then there have been many changes. The
revolution is no longer the affair of young people.
But the question of how to unite the scattered
members of Russian opposition remains, as it was
then, the question of the day. We may even say
that it is now more pressing than ever before. In
any case the discussions and writings on this
favourite theme of ours are now more serious and
better suited to the real needs of the case than
formerly.

The revolutionary cycle which began with that
movement of the young generation as a mass, of
which we have spoken, is evidently ended. Something new will now begin, but what no one can say
beforehand. Only one thing is certain—that the
coming movement will be wider than the former

one was. It has become clear to every one that revolutionists *by speciality*—"Nihilists," as they are called in western Europe—cannot alone overthrow the autocracy, however great may be their energy and heroism.

The revolution must be widened. But how? To whom must we look for support for it? This is the question about which programmes are drawn up, over which parties split into fractions, and newspapers come into and pass out of existence.

Russia is a land of peasants. And yet, so far as we know, there is not at this moment a single section among the Russian revolutionists which seriously looks to the peasantry for support—that is, which really works to obtain partizans among them. The revolutionary party, having found the hopes it had built upon the peasants so illusive eighteen years ago, evidently fears to appeal to them again. But during this long period the peasants have had time to undergo a momentous change. Twenty years of change and mental development, of district commanders, sectarianism, famine, want of land, and robbery, have not passed without leaving traces.

A new attempt to "go among the people," though, of course, not in the old way and not with the old message, but with a practical and comprehensible plan of a transfer of the land by the state to the people, and of peasant autonomy—such an attempt

3

would have, we believe, a good chance to meet with
a quite other response and to give quite other results
from those obtained by the attempts of the seventies.

But such a party does not yet exist, though it will
probably spring up in the natural course of the
movement's growth, or at the first widespread signs
of upheaval among the people. Up till now our
movement is exclusively an urban one, depending
upon certain elements of the town population—
partly on the working-classes, but chiefly upon
the educated class in general.

Our revolutionary party splits up into two divisions
in accordance with this fact. A minority, the Russian
Social Democrats, or, to speak more accurately, The
Society for the Emancipation of Labour (as we are
all Social Democrats), who have grouped themselves
round the well-known Geneva periodical, see only
one possible support for the revolution—the factory
workmen, the proletariat now growing up in Russia.

That our town workmen present a most favourable
soil in which to implant political and social ideas
every one will agree who knows anything of that
very promising class. Any serious work among
them results in valuable additions to our revolutionary strength. Town workmen are more responsive and easier to approach than peasants, and
possess the enormous advantage that their every-
day life, containing as it does more intellectual and

exciting elements than that of the peasants, does not choke the seed cast among them, but strengthens and encourages its growth. We know of cases in which a propagandist, coming to a factory absolutely unknown to him, unexpectedly meets with " a treasure trove " of revolutionist workmen, who prove to be either disciples or disciples of disciples of some other propagandist who worked there six or eight years before. Several such cases have become publicly known, thanks to disturbances among the workmen and the trials resulting therefrom. The peasant class, unfortunately, does not show such examples.

We sympathise deeply with the attempt of which we have spoken, to increase the movement among the town workmen. But to see in them the chief lever by means of which the autocracy is to be overthrown, is to lose sight, while looking at theories, of the real state of things in Russia.

Whether the factory workmen be one million only, as the official statistics declare, or three, or even four millions, as the *Social Democrat* says, the case remains the same.

Undoubtedly the numerical strength of the town working class is not great, and, considering how little education that class possesses, how scattered it is, and how utterly lacking in any conscious class-feeling, it is impossible to speak seriously, at the present time, of its playing an independent political part; and, above all, of its leading the movement. At present this class can be nothing more than a help to the revolutionary movement. The principal support, without any question, is the educated class.

This view is held, if not in words, at least in practice, by the majority of Russian revolutionists, from the old "Narodnaya Volia" to its latest adherents; and on this point we fully agree with them.

After the peasantry, the educated class is certainly the most powerful in the State. It commands the Tzar's army and fleet, and might, with one successful military plot, hew down the autocracy at its very root.

The educated class has given us Jeliabov, Kibalchich, Perovskaya, and many others, and will always give successors to them and continuers of their work, because it is the heart of the nation, which feels more intensely than any other class the nation's wrongs and sufferings, and more passionately believes in its bright and glorious future. Moreover, this same educated class occupies all the high posts, and fulfils all the most important social functions. It manages the press, sits in the Zemstvos and municipal councils, and holds the university professorships.

The educated class is an enormous power in the

land. Moreover, this class is thoroughly permeated with discontent, and, above all, with conscious discontent, as it fully understands what is the cause of its troubles. If all those who at heart loathe the autocracy could make up their minds to attack it openly, it could not stand for five months.

But how is this powerful class to be persuaded to take a more active part in the struggle for the liberation of Russia ? How are we to clear away the lingering distrust still somewhat felt towards the party which has taken upon itself the initiative in that struggle ? We say " somewhat," because, since the time when the " Narodnaya Volia " raised the banner of political strife, the position has materially changed. The attitude of the general mass of educated Russian society towards the revolutionary movement is at the present time very different from that of fifteen years ago. But for all that, the movement is still far from having spread throughout all those strata of society on whose support it ought to reckon. And now there is arising among Russian revolutionists a desire to work towards a common understanding.

This desire has found expression in a whole series of publications produced abroad. But we will speak of only one—the Geneva paper *Svobodnaya Rossiya*, in which this tendency is shown in its extremest and most characteristic form.

Starting from the hypothesis (in our opinion a

mistaken one) that our Liberals shrink from the socialism of the revolutionary party, some of our comrades in this paper propose to "temporarily" entirely conceal their socialism, and, also "temporarily," to become Liberals.

The Geneva organ of this group has done good service in that it, first of all the papers issued by refugees, put forward certain useful and elementary truths, which, however, were regarded by some people as dreadful heresy. For this step it deserves, if not the thanks of posterity, at least the indulgence of its contemporaries. Nevertheless, we cannot refrain from saying that its proposed plan of pruning ourselves down and hiding ourselves away is one which cannot bear even the mildest criticism, either from the theoretical or from the practical point of view.

Socialism is the greatest moral force at work in modern society, and to hide its light under a bushel or in any way to weaken its power in Russia would be to wilfully destroy the very thing that is the life and soul of our movement.

A struggle such as ours depends entirely upon self-sacrifice, upon the capacity of separate individuals to give up their life, their liberty, everything for the happiness of their country. The deeper, wider, and more universal the idea of this potential happiness, the sooner will awake and the louder will speak in human hearts the mighty social instinct. No man will immolate himself for the sake of, say, an extension of local autonomy or any other such reform, however beneficial. But thousands of people have willingly died when the belief grew up in them that the happiness of humanity would be bought by their death.

A hundred, even fifty, years ago, the idea of political liberty had power to arouse this faith in masses of men, and our political crisis would have passed over more quickly and more easily had it happened then. But that time is gone, and cannot be recalled. The formulæ of political liberty have lost their magical power over men's hearts. That power is now possessed by socialism, and, we believe, is possessed by it in as much greater degree as its doctrine is completer, more scientific, and more concrete than the political metaphysics of the last century. Even from an objective point of view, apart from the question of liking or disliking socialism, all opponents of the Russian autocracy ought to desire the widest possible spread of socialism in Russia, for the imperial absolutism has no more dangerous enemy.

The very energy of the revolutionary struggle evidently depends upon the attitude of the Russian educated class towards socialism, and we attribute the present comparative lull to the dying away of the fresh influx of socialist ideas. Instead of the wide, inspiring study of great social questions, on which the former revolutionary generation grew up, the young people of the present day have perforce to content themselves with turning over and piecing together old, musty "programmes."

Undoubtedly this blank will be filled up, and, we hope, soon. Undoubtedly the rapid development of socialism in the West will sooner or later be reflected in Russia; every new wave of socialism flings drops of the living water across the frontier into Russia, causing there a ferment, a lifting up of spirit, a growth of social feeling, which cannot fail to result in a strengthening of the political revolt.

But we must meet this natural influence half-way, consciously introducing into our life that which is being brought into it by the natural course of events.

There can be no question of any putting aside of socialist work for the sake of any connections whatever. Before talking of union, the party must take care to become a power with which it will be worth while to unite. And if we spent less time upon discussions about unity and uniting, and worked at that which is under our hands, each of us in his own sphere, according to his own tendencies, capacities, and even accidental position, our powers would be far greater than they are now; we should have friends and allies everywhere, and the beginning of the end would be nearer by many years than it seems to be now.

But whether it be in consequence of our intolerance, which renders differences of opinion insufferable to us, or whether in consequence of our passion for revolutionary dogmatism, our "cause" still continues to be a mere cloud of words cast upon the wind. In one town you will find two philosophers who agree with each other on every point except some fifth wheel in the revolutionary cart. One would have thought that when once they are convinced that their difference is one which cannot be got over, nothing would be simpler than for them to peacefully part, and either take up practical work for themselves, or gird up their loins and go each his own way among indifferent and blinded men, who have never heard the new word, and prepare the soil by winning over new adherents. But the philosophers prefer to go to each other's houses and spend days, weeks, months in fruitless discussions about the everlasting fifth wheel, until the noise they make attracts the police, who swoop down and march them off to the Yakuts to finish their argument in the open air. And if the two philosophers have collected round themselves each a little band of friends, the friends then continue to visit each other, to carry on the same discussions and repeat the same commonplaces, with the inevitable "draw-

ing up of general programmes" and "plans of
unification," and all the customary revolutionary
mill-round, until the police swoop down again to
wind up the business this time with a general raid.

Three-fourths of our available and precious forces
perish in this way, and yet it is surely easy to see
that a change of tactics would be advantageous,
not only to the general cause, but even to the
beloved fifth wheel itself.   Not from frivolity or
shallowness, but just from passionate devotion to
the cause and desire to serve it in any way, Russians more than any other race follow successful
examples.   There is, perhaps, no path upon which
they would not enter, however difficult, however
terrible it might be, no action from which they
would shrink, if they could only see plainly that
such a path or such an action would really lead to
the awakening of Russia from her age-long sleep, or
would be a real menace to the age-long tyranny.
Things which yesterday were condemned are looked
upon to-day as new revelations.   The Byzantine
dogmatism is forgotten ; enemies of not long ago
become impassioned adherents ; and the disor-
ganised crowd of yesterday, fired with a common
enthusiasm, becomes to-day a phalanx of Titans,
ready to take by storm heaven itself.   Historical
instances are not far to seek : it was not by argu-
ments, not by the completeness of its theories, but

by the fascination of its actions, that the old Narodnaya Volya gathered around itself all that was most energetic in revolutionary Russia.

But let us return to our subject.

What we have said about the tactics as regards each other of separate revolutionary subdivisions, is applicable also to the relations between the various parties of the opposition. For the sake of our common cause we must make it our first care to render our party a power in the land. And how can any party become a power, which is afraid openly to acknowledge its own convictions, which puts on an artificial meekness in order to win over or to please this person or that?

And, indeed, what is the use of all these efforts, which deceive no one, to hide our candle under a bushel? We ought long ago to have given up the habit, borrowed from Western Europe, of confusing Liberalism with narrow bourgeois class-interest. Ours is not a class opposition, but an intellectual opposition. Modern Russia, which so often reminds us of France before the Revolution, in no other respect so closely resembles her as in the humanitarian and profoundly democratic feeling of her privileged class. One must wear very thick spectacles indeed if he cannot see that our " Liberals " are, by their opinions, very different from those of the West in our day. The majority of them are advocates of most radical economic reforms, and a large number sympathise, in essentials, with socialism. Where is the danger, here, of "frightening" them with our socialism ?

There are, of course, in Russia chemically pure Liberals, Manchesterites ; but we do not believe that even they would turn away from us for our socialism.

It is one thing not to agree with socialism, and quite another thing to wish to deprive socialists of the right to preach their doctrine as freely as other parties. The English Liberals are, indeed, we may say universally, opponents on principle of socialism, and yet they not only do not attempt to shut the mouths of their socialists, but even defend them when any aggression is made upon their rights. The entire Liberal press took the part of the socialists at the time of the once-famous Dodd Street case, when the police tried to prevent the socialists from holding meetings at that place, and the most eminent of the militant opponents of socialism, the late Charles Bradlaugh, made an interpellation in Parliament about the case. And this was by no means a demonstration of generosity to an enemy, but a simple expression, which astonished no one, of that feeling of civil solidarity and civil liberty which has become second nature to all English people.

Is it possible that we are so hopelessly, so barbarously behind the age that these elementary truths, which ordinary English shopkeepers, cabmen, and cotton spinners, regard as the alphabet of political education, are incomprehensible to our picked men, our Liberals, among whom are hundreds of professors, writers, and savants, some of them of European fame?

If there are, indeed, among our malcontents, any persons who, even now, at this time of general, intolerable oppression, indulge in dreams of gagging their opponents with anti-socialist statutes and martial law, what sort of Liberals are they? and are they worth taking into account? The sooner and the more thoroughly we repel them, the better for us and for the cause of Russian liberty.

We repeat : socialism is not, and never has been, the hindrance to the uniting of the Russian opposition ; that hindrance must be sought in the political, not the economic side of our programme—so far as programmes play any part in the matter at all.

The putting forward of political revolt as a means towards further development, was for us a decisive step in advance. But from the formal point of view it was a retrogression from a more extreme, though less definite programme, and we have still not got rid of a phraseology which makes it appear as if we looked upon that step as a kind of "falling into sin."

When we speak of our desire to obtain political liberty, we think it necessary to add, as it were in self-justification, that we want it not for itself, but as a means towards the solving of the social question.

We all understand quite well that, in contemporary Russia, political liberty can be obtained only in the form of a constitutional monarchy. Up till now the world has invented no other form of free state except Constitutional Monarchy or Republic, and so far no voices have been raised for a republic in Russia. And yet we still continue to look upon the word "constitution" as something unclean. We carefully avoid the use of it, employing various roundabout methods of speech, for fear people should "confuse us with" the constitutionalists. We become bitterly angry if any one of our number calls things by their real names.

But why all these fig-leaves? We prefer a republican form of government to any other, and most certainly have no prejudice in favour of the Romanov dynasty. But once we consider it inexpedient, or not worth while to try to overthrow it, we prefer to say so frankly, and therefore we put forward, as our immediate aim, the winning of a constitution for Russia.

Finally—and this is the most important point—

while preaching the principle of the supreme right of the nation to decide all questions of state; while repeatedly declaring that the violent actions to which we now have recourse, are purely temporary measures, which will give place to peaceful, intellectual work as soon as popular representation is substituted for the present despotism—while acknowledging all this, we, at the same time, cannot give up our revolutionary rhetoric and continue to talk of our "revolutionary" socialism and of "the social revolution without explaining whether we mean these expressions to be understood in the literal or metaphorical sense.

For our part we object to this ambiguity and confusion. We recognise the expressions above quoted only in the broad philosophical sense in which Lassalle accepted them. But as they are usually understood in another sense, we prefer to leave them aside altogether.

We absolutely and categorically distinguish between the two divisions of our tactics: the political division and the economic.

We believe that the worthless gang which now rules over Russia, taking advantage of a misunderstanding of the peasant masses, can be overthrown only by force, and to this end we see no other means than force. In politics we are revolutionists, recognising not only popular insurrection, but military plots, nocturnal attacks upon the palace, bombs and dynamite. We shall not, while living abroad, preach these things to our Russian comrades. Apart from the moral impossibility of inciting others to actions in which we ourselves can take no part, there is also the question of the timeliness, and, therefore, of the expediency, of a given action— a question which can be decided only on the spot.

But we regard all such acts as morally justifiable, and we are ready to defend them and acknowledge our moral solidarity with them, once people have been driven to commit them. In view of the cynical, boundless despotism now rampant in Russia, every form of protest is lawful, and there are outrages upon human nature so intolerable that violence becomes the moral duty of the citizens.

But as regards the introduction of socialism into life, we are evolutionists. We utterly disbelieve in the possibility of reconstructing economic relation-ships by means of a burst of revolutionary inspira-tion. That is a huge work which needs great mental efforts on the part of many people, much preparation, much practical experience and correc-tion, and therefore much time.

We could prove, by quoting what have now become historical documents, that those who at one time really were "the party," regarded the realisation of socialism just as a peaceful intellectual work. · But we will dispense with quotations. We have cast off the authority of ancient tradition for the right of the individual reason to judge of and decide all questions in heaven and earth. Let us then reverence our past, but let us not forge for ourselves new chains and reintroduce the forgotten cultus of tradition. Let us look upon the matter with our own eyes, and answer the question whether, general considerations apart, there is any logic in the uniting of revolutionary socialism with that struggle for representative government which is now taking place on Russian soil? Is it not clear that a free state has incomparably more power than an autocracy to repress disturbances of a political character? The latter depends solely upon the police and the army; the former will have at its disposal the same police and army plus—and think what a plus!—the support of the whole nation. Why, then, substitute a powerful enemy for a weak one? Would it not be simpler to return to anarchist theories, and, taking advantage of the moment, raise at once the standard of rebellion?

It is only from the point of view of evolutionary socialism that the struggle against autocracy, with its numberless and terrible sacrifices, has a true and great significance; otherwise it is nothing but an aimless and sanguinary farce—strife for strife's sake, practice in self-sacrifice.

4

But the logic of life has proved stronger than the logic of our heads. From the time when the question of political revolution became the principal question of the moment, the anarchist theories, which up till then had prevailed among us, were replaced by the ideas of social democracy. To anarchists, representative government is not worth fighting for, and, therefore, there are no anarchists in Russia.

Would it not be wiser to bring our programme into harmony with our activity?

We believe that political liberty gives all that is needed for the solution of the social question. If we look at the West, we see clearly to what brilliant results our comrades have attained by using those weapons of propaganda and agitation which constitutional freedom has placed in their hands. We also see that the more powerful becomes the socialist party in a land, the more complete is the victory of evolutionary socialism. In proportion as the results obtained are more precious, as the moment comes nearer when the party may expect to be called to the practical realisation of its ideals, the complications and difficulties of the gigantic task become more evident, and the rhetoric of blood and violence inherited from political revolutions is more decisively abandoned. The German socialist party, which has astonished the world with its titanic growth, presents the most brilliant example of political discretion and self-control.

Profiting by its experience, we propose to take our stand openly in favour of evolutionary socialism, recognising freedom of speech, freedom of the press, and universal franchise as fully sufficient weapons ; and, so long as they are guaranteed by inviolable law, the only right weapons to use in the coming social struggle.

But while regarding the solution of the labour question in Russia as a problem which will be brought prominently forward in perhaps the near future, we emphatically protest against the habit which has grown up among us of treating political liberty exclusively as a means to "the solution of the social question." We feel as an insult the idea that we should look upon liberty as a mere tool with which to obtain something else, as though the needs and feelings of free men were strange to us, as though our duties to the people have blinded us to our duties to ourselves and our human dignity.

We think, moreover, that this timid phrase may lay us open to a danger, the possibility of which is probably unsuspected by many of the wise persons who repeat it. From the constant harnessing, as it were on principle, of political freedom to the solution of the labour question, there is but one step to democratic imperialism. From the point of view of narrow labour interests, it may appear more advantageous to uphold the huge power already established, once it offers immediate economic reforms, than to follow the long and difficult path to general freedom. We may be answered that only very short-sighted persons could fall into this trap. But unhappily such short-sightedness is a common disease among Russians, and this fact renders caution doubly necessary. We admit of no compromise on this point, and, in case of a conflict between civil liberty and imperial socialism, we should take our stand on the side of "bourgeois" Liberals against the "peasantist" socialists, who allowed themselves to be caught in such a snare.

We do not believe in the possibility of making the people prosperous by decrees and edicts from above. And both imperial and Jacobinical socialism lead to the same result : the transformation of the country into a huge workhouse.

Only where there exists general freedom and where the whole people can judge of and decide upon social matters, is it possible to practically realise in life any new ideas or principles, including the reconstruction of economic relations on the basis of socialism. By the "people" we mean, not merely the representatives of physical labour but the whole nation. Therefore we desire the spread of liberty throughout the length and breadth of the country, that every social organisation should be permeated by it from centre to periphery. We desire autonomy, local and regional; we desire a federalism which will render independent all those races and lands which make up the state. We desire freedom for all Russians without distinction of party; and we are ready to defend it in the name of that universal sense of civic solidarity which lies outside of class-questions, and which exists in all advanced countries in proportion to the degree of their advancement. To repudiate it for the sake of any economic philosophy, even of German origin, would be as unreasonable as to deny the existence of mutual insurance companies on the ground that all men are egotists.

It is only by guaranteeing liberty to our opponents that we can secure our own. The science of liberty does not consist in knowing how to do and say what is pleasant or advantageous to ourselves—every one can manage that without learning how—but in developing the faculty of tolerating what is unpleasant or even injurious, whenever it is the result of the use of rights equal to our own.

We do not see why all persons of a progressive turn of mind who are our opponents on the economic questions should not pay us back in the same coin. There is not in our view a single point which could hinder us from working in common with them.

We acknowledge without equivocation that, as regards the political question, which for us is the question of the day, our programme is just that of the advanced section of Russian Liberals, as it has been stated in the foreign press, and, to such an extent as the censorship has allowed, in a few Russian periodicals. We should not hesitate to say that we subscribe and accept their programme, did we not know that really we have taken it from the same source from which they took it : observation of European life and study of European political history.

The Russian revolutionists, in consequence of the peculiar conditions under which their movement was born, protested for a long time, as we have said, against " politics " ; and when at last they accepted it, they avoided the beaten track and, wishing to find out for themselves something new and original, went by roundabout bypaths according to the proverb : "Five miles straight, but perhaps three miles round."

The Liberals, on the contrary, went straight towards their end without any hair-splitting, and thus attained to a simpler, more logical, and more practical standpoint in politics.

In offering our suggestions to our Russian comrades we have laid aside all considerations of political opportunism, such as the desire to "attract" the Liberals. Undoubtedly it is both desirable and important to avoid all causes of mis-understanding and mutual distrust between the two great branches of our opposition. But it is still more desirable and important, for the sake of the party itself, to set our foundation straight, as it were, to get rid of all confusion of ideas; for such confusion may, in the future if not now, become a source of misunderstandings, errors, and even failure.

As for the question of the suggested leaguing together of Liberals and revolutionists, we hasten to explain that we are not contemplating any formal or organic unification. We hold, in contradiction to the general opinion, that a true organic league between us and the Liberals will become possible, not before the revolution, but, to use the common term, "on the day after" it. To hope that, in a moment and by one blow, we can win for ourselves as much liberty as is enjoyed by the English and Americans, would be too *naïve*. There is far more reason to suppose that our first portion of liberty will be a much smaller one, and that it will become widened later on by the common efforts of all pro-gressive parties. Until that time there can be no question of a common organisation; attempts at it can lead to nothing but fruitless destruction. The parties must remain separate, independent wholes,

joining together for special practical actions, but
without amalgamating, like diversely equipped
troops forming one army. The Liberal party
cannot, if only because of its size, adopt those
methods of action which are suitable for revolutionists.

A general league between the parties at the
present time can be only a moral one, based on
mutual comprehension and trust, and on the consciousness of common interests. It is for such a
league that we wish to make a way by removing
some of the imaginary obstacles. And here, too,
we would choose practice rather than theory, and
application to life rather than abstract propositions.
It is for us a matter of comparative indifference
whether any of our suggestions shall or shall not
enter into any of the numerous home-made "programmes" concocted every year in various holes
and corners of our huge country. Everything that
has entered into life must necessarily, sooner or
later, find its way into a programme; but much
that stands in programmes will for ever remain a
dead letter in life.

What we fervently desire is that our words may
contribute, in however small a degree, to the development amongst us of greater mutual tolerance,
and especially to the abandoning of the absurd
attitude towards all persons called Liberals, which

has become customary among revolutionists. Our party pride and narrowness, our constant drawing of distinctions between "ours" and "yours," with a tacit assumption that we are made of finer clay, have done more to cause dissensions among us than all the programmes put together.

And it is useless for us to disguise this foolish self-laudation under a mask of devotion to the cause or strictness of principle. Principles have nothing to do with the matter. As for "the cause," it has become a shame and a sorrow to think of. The autocracy has descended upon everything that is alive in Russia like a leaden coffin-lid. Never before has even our unhappy land lived through so dark and dreadful a time. After a short period of stupefaction, the autocracy has evidently determined to revenge itself for the humiliation of two years' captivity, for the hesitation caused by terror, and for its momentary consent to compromise. And it has succeeded. It triumphs, and no one resists it. Serfdom, with its most monstrous attributes, has been practically reintroduced. A gang of official brigands does what it pleases with Russia ; and the whips and rods of the police flourish over Russian heads, in town and country, in prison and street, in the police stations of the capital, and in far-off Siberia. Things inconceivable, intolerable, that can hardly be spoken of aloud, are done, and done with impunity. In face of this boundless humiliation, of this insolent and deliberate outrage upon everything that is sacred to us, shall there not awake in us the direct and simple sense of indignation? Shall it not sweep away as dust both the dry bones of dogmatism and all petty quarrels and dissensions, and show us a comrade and a brother in every man who is an enemy of our enemy, and who is willing to take part in the fight? It is only by our dissensions, by our incapacity to work together, that the present system is enabled to stand; and unless we can attain to political coherency and learn to act in unison, it will continue to stand for years and years.

SUPPLEMENT.

THE BEGINNING OF THE END.

The present pamphlet was written more than half a year ago; [1] and, its publication having been unavoidably delayed, it now appears under conditions materially different from those under which it was written. During this period the autocracy has received a blow from which it cannot recover, and which may possibly shake it to its very foundations. We speak of the terrible famine which has fallen upon almost the whole of corn-growing Russia.

[1] In January, 1891.

Men have proved powerless and incompetent to
snatch the country out of the hands of the autocracy
before it was too late ; and now Nature has risen up
to do the work with her blind and merciless agent,
hunger, which assuredly will sweep away a hundred
times more lives and cause a hundred times more
suffering than the most sanguinary revolution.

This is not a pleasant reflection. But once the
fact is so, it behoves us to think what we shall do
to render a repetition of such misfortunes impossible
in future.

It is needless to explain that the present famine
is the inevitable consequence of that condition of
chronic destitution to which the people had been
reduced before the beginning of this black year.
That is now acknowledged and repeated throughout
the whole Russian press, and the very Government
dares not deny it. It is also superfluous to demon-
strate that the present crisis cannot pass over with
the current year, but is certain to spread itself over
many coming years, gradually shaking to pieces the
state machinery, bringing the finances into hopeless
confusion, and driving the Government into material
and moral bankruptcy. Already twenty-five (by
some calculations, thirty-four) millions of peasants
—that is to say, over a third of the taxpayers—are
hopelessly ruined, possessing no longer either cattle
seed-corn, or any other means upon which to exist

and to pay taxes. The necessity of supporting them, and of somehow filling up the deficit in the budget, must necessarily result in completing the ruin of the other two-thirds who are still contriving to somehow make both ends meet. The year 1892 threatens to be still darker than the present year, and we see no prospect of improvement in the future.

The most favourable atmospheric conditions cannot produce corn on an unsown field, or render it possible for the peasants to plough without cattle. The position is a hopeless one, and we may indeed look upon the present crisis as the beginning of the end. All this is plain to see for any one capable of looking further into the future than to-morrow. We have spoken of this in order to warn those whom our words may reach from exaggerating the political effects of external elemental forces, among which must be classed such crises as the present one.

We remember how, ten years ago, the enormous and apparently invincible energy of the revolutionists, with the executive committee at their head, favoured the growth, in certain circles, of a peculiar kind of cowardice. People who, in all other respects, were reasonable and well meaning would put forward, as an excuse for their own inactivity, their belief in the power of the revolutionists. " They will smash up the autocracy," said these enthusiasts; and considered that to offer help to such Titans would be quite superfluous. There are people ready to transfer this lazy optimism to famine, to an unsuccessful war, and to other such blind forces.

This is a pitiful mistake. Neither war nor famine will make a revolution for us, or destroy the autocracy. Economic confusion may bring the state into a condition of complete bankruptcy, of incapacity to pay the salaries of its officers and officials, may cause the entire loss of its credit; and yet the despotism may remain unshaken, as has happened in the case of Turkey. A war may reduce Russia to the position of a third-rate Power without necessarily destroying the autocracy. Nay, famine may call forth a whole series of petty popular revolts and disturbances, which may be each time suppressed, and may end in nothing but the useless slaughter of now hundreds, now thousands of rebels. Peasant revolts are a mere elemental force, which, alone and without the help of a conscious opposition, cannot change anything containing an idea, be it even a worn-out one.

We do not say that the upheaval of elemental forces, should it take place, will subside leaving no results. On the contrary, we are convinced that this will not be the case, just because such an outburst of elemental discontent would certainly awaken to life and activity the representatives of a conscious opposition. We only wish to point out that for us there is no salvation without a conscious revolution. Therefore the most energetic activity on the part of the conscious opposition is not merely a means of "hastening events," as the partisans of "organic development" like to express themselves, but a *conditio sine quâ non* of the very occurrence of such events.

What are those to do who wish to alleviate the misery of the people by word and deed, irrespective of possible consequences to themselves?

At present famine rages in the country districts only; and in several cases those districts have already witnessed active expressions of popular misery and despair. Is not the place of the revolutionists now in the country? and should they not turn their energies towards the direct incitement of the peasants to insurrection?

Educated and determined persons may do great service to the popular movement already beginning, by organising it and giving to it greater energy and stability and a wider reach. But it is not probable that revolutionists can have much success as initiators and arousers of such movements. And this, not because the work is too great for their powers, but because it demands means and weapons different in character from those at our disposal. We cannot spread rumours of " Enoch having come to life again," or of a " horse having fallen from the sky with mystic inscriptions on its back." Still less can we circulate tales of mysterious imperial edicts. Yet such fables, which excite the popular imagination, are always at the bottom of peasant insurrections. It is possible that this year's famine may not provoke any widespread peasant disturbances; and even if it should do so, they will have to be the work of the peasants themselves, not of revolutionists. Our forces are chiefly in the towns; and there, without being compelled to resort to fables and inventions, we can organise a direct, energetic, fully conscious attack which may give the death-blow to the shaken autocracy. Shaken it undoubtedly will be by the present crisis, whether that crisis bring about a peasant war or not. We do not speak of the non-payment of taxes; the starving people cannot remain quiet, either in the villages or in the towns, to which the famine-stricken masses flock. The central Government will thus become weakened and its conscious opponents will be able to overthrow it more easily than at any other time. Thus it was in the French Revolution, and thus it must be in our case.

By what means and in what way the attack
should be made is a question of tactics which can
only be decided by persons on the spot. All that
we can say is that only a widespread movement,
supported, as far as possible, by the whole mass
of the discontented, can succeed, and that this
moment is peculiarly favourable for such a movement.

We may compare the present position to defeat
in a war with an external enemy. The terrible
scourge of famine has been brought upon the
country by the Government ; for, under other
conditions, no failure of crops could have caused
anything resembling the present misery. And this
same Government now shows itself utterly incapable
of helping the people in their distress; it has acknowledged this fact before the whole country, and has
handed over the task to private initiative. Yet, at
the same time, so great is its fear of the public exercising any control over it, that it places in the way
of such initiative obstacles which render any real
help impossible. Neither Russian society nor those
foreigners who have shown themselves willing to
bring their millions to the aid of the Russian people
care to trust their funds to the uncontrolled disposal
of the Russian bureaucracy. Tens of thousands,
maybe hundreds of thousands, of Russians are
doomed to perish because the Government, which

has refused to help them itself, is afraid to let others do so.

Such a spectacle is intolerable to all in whom everything human has not withered up. The discontent grows more and more intense, and is becoming universal, spreading through all spheres of society, sowing dissension and confusion in the ranks of the Government itself, terrifying it and paralysing its energy. Anything may be done at such moments if only the opposition prove capable of organising the discontent.

The only way out of the present desperate position is to convoke a general National Assembly, invested with full powers. Such an assembly could put an end to political and economic chaos and could give to the forces of the nation room for general development and a more rational application to all spheres of labour and thought. Nothing but the introduction of popular representation can put a stop to the chronic starvation, financial entanglement, and lawlessness which now prevail in Russia. This is recognised by every one except the Government, which still thinks only of how to prolong its shameful existence by fair means or foul.

True, even if not elected, representatives of the people must compel the Government to lay down its arms, by moral pressure, by the imposing strength of the masses gathered round the standard of constitution, and also by force. We should be glad to find ourselves mistaken, but we do not think that our Government will yield until it has exhausted all means of resistance, and this will force the opposition to employ all means in the struggle. Neither the Liberals nor the revolutionists separately can overthrow the autocracy. There must be large and energetic demonstrations, declarations, protests, from the town and county councils, from the press and from society; it is absolutely essential that there be also a free organ to act as a mirror of the movement; but it is doubtful whether such efforts can bring about the desired end without direct attacks, without military and other plots, which would force the Government to seek refuge in timely compromises.

The pledge of victory is the mutual support of both sections of the opposition. Therefore our last word to all friends of the Russian people must be an appeal to lay aside all sectarian differences for the sake of the things we all demand, to join together and to fight. Let us fight on the largest scale that is open to us, but in any case let us fight, whatever be the difficulties or the sacrifices.

The terrible disasters through which our country is passing lay upon us great obligations, and upon our way of fulfilling them it depends whether Russia shall enter into the twentieth century as a free country, or whether, degenerating, falling to pieces, losing her national features, she must shamefully wait until the march of European progress flings to her, as an alms, what other nations have conquered for themselves by heroism and self-sacrifice.

THE AGITATION ABROAD.

I.

In December, 1889, at a small private meeting of only four persons, two English and two Russians, it was determined to found in England a society, with the object of helping forward the cause of Russian emancipation by all means legitimate for foreigners.

Taking into consideration the English dread of "responsibility," and consequent dislike of interfering in anything which they do not thoroughly understand, we might have supposed the success of the project to be very doubtful. But one of the two English persons was Robert Spence Watson, now President of the Liberal Federation of Great Britain, one of the most influential and gifted Englishmen of our time. To his fresh and living enthusiasm for the Russian cause, to his energy and the powerful fascination of his personality, we owe it that, in little more than two months, dozens of the most respected names in England were written down in the list of members of the new society.

The motives which induced Dr. Spence Watson (a man no longer young and as busy as only English statesmen are) to take up the Russian agitation are so characteristic, and the further success of the agitation is so largely his work, that it may be worth while to say a few words about him personally.

Dr. Spence Watson is a Newcastle man, a lawyer of radical convictions. He comes of an old family, which belonged to the Society of Friends, and has long been distinguished for its fervent sympathy with the cause of liberty in all countries and for all nations. His father was a strong reformer, a friend of John Bright and Lloyd Garrison, and Dr. Watson himself, having come under the personal influence of Kossuth, Garibaldi, and Felice Orsini, at the age of twenty, was much inclined to fling over the Quaker's unconditional objection to war and join Garibaldi's "Thousand" which landed in Sicily in 1860. Ten years later, at the time of the Franco-Prussian war, he collected a large sum of money for the relief of the French peasants ruined by the war, and, without waiting for the promulgation of peace, went out to the scene of hostilities to distribute the funds in person. This form of philanthropy proved to be almost more dangerous than direct participation in the fighting. He had more to fear from friends than from enemies. On several occasions he nearly lost his life because the French imagined him to be a

Prussian spy who had come under the pretext of philanthropy to examine their position.

In 1877, during the Russo-Turkish war, he was an ardent partisan of Russia, as, like Mr. Gladstone, he then believed that the Russian Government really desired to free Bulgaria. His great influence in the north of England counted for much in bringing about that revulsion of English public opinion and political action which followed the famous disclosures of the " Bulgarian Atrocities."

A man with such antecedents and with sympathies so wide could not fail to be interested in the sudden outburst of internal discontent in Russia itself, that Russian revolutionary movement which in Western Europe has been dubbed " Nihilism." When a series of publications appeared in the English language explaining the meaning and aim of this struggle, the position of the people, the mutual relations of Government and society, that interest gradually grew into profound sympathy. Such sympathy does not necessarily imply complete solidarity, but renders impossible all narrowness of view, and enables men to rise above prejudices and dissensions and to understand by simple human feeling all that is great and noble in a movement such as ours.

The publication of Mr. Kennan's Siberian articles was the last touch which converted this feeling into an overpowering impulse to do something to relieve, in however slight a degree, the miseries that had produced so deep an impression.

At one of the preliminary meetings of the future Society, Dr. Watson, speaking of his resolve to give some practical expression to his sympathy with the cause of Russian freedom, said, " We cannot remain indifferent spectators of the cruelties that are inflicted upon our neighbours in Russia. We must help in some way, however little may be the help that we can give. For us this is a question of duty and of conscience; for some of us it is a question of our peace of mind."

In answer to this appeal was formed, in 1890, the Society of Friends of Russian Freedom, with a committee consisting of twenty-eight members. The committee now contains ten members of Parliament and several leaders of the Radical party, such as Professor Stuart, Mr. Burt, Mr. Allanson Picton, and others. On the committee list we also find such names as Stopford Brooke, Percy Bunting, Charles Berry, Mrs. Mallet, &c. The first and most difficult step was taken. In the following year, 1891, the organisation spread to America, where another society was formed resembling the English one in aims and character, and with as influential a committee.

In this manner the Russian work abroad was first formulated and organised. Both societies, from their

very beginning, have kept before them definite aims
and a clear understanding of what means they judge
fit to use for the attainment of those aims.

Neither society confines itself to protesting against
special instances of Russian tyranny, such as the
Siberian horrors and the brutal treatment of political
prisoners in exile, although these are the things
which make the strongest impression upon foreigners.
The societies hold a wider view of their work ; and,
believing that the root of the mischief lies in the
autocracy itself, have set before themselves as an
aim the support from without of those who are
fighting against the autocracy within the country.

This more radical attitude of the societies towards
the Russian question shows a fuller understanding
on the part of foreigners of the true position of
Russia. Simultaneously with the founding of the
English society, another society, with as wide a
programme, was started in Denver, in the far
west of America, on the initiative of Mr. Scott
Saxon, an enthusiast in Russian affairs. At the
present time, in both England and America, one
may meet everywhere persons who feel in this way
towards Russian affairs.

Far more complex is the question : How can
practical help be given ?

The struggle for liberty, wherever it takes place,
always meet with sympathy and support among free

peoples. When matters reach the length of open insurrection that sympathy and support express themselves in a very simple manner, by the collection of funds for the war and by the enlisting of volunteers. Foreign volunteers took part with the Americans in their War of Independence; with the Greeks and Slavs every time those races rose against Turkey; with the Poles in their insurrections, and with Garibaldi in all his campaigns. Foreign volunteers would certainly join us too, should any Russian Garibaldi raise the standard of armed insurrection.

Open insurrection is a kind of plebiscite to which all the nation is called to decide by siding with the one party or the other, what kind of social order it prefers. But so long as the fight is carried on by means of plots and secret societies, over which the nation has no direct control, foreigners have no place in it. Only Russians can uphold, before the face of the country and before that part of society on which retaliation on the part of the Government weighs most heavily, the supreme right of men in a no-thoroughfare. We mean the right of every man to defend himself and his own, his honour, his life, and his human dignity by any means possible, whatever be the results of them, when less objectionable means of self-defence are rendered impossible. Only Russians, fighting in

the name of the people and taking upon themselves
to decide what the people need and wish, can offer
not only a warrant of sincerity which is testified by
their readiness to sacrifice their own lives, but also
the warrant of competency to understand the needs
and conditions of life of the land for which they are
fighting.

All these considerations, suggested by simple
respect for the rights and dignity of the Russian
people, were thought of when the programme of the
new society was drawn up. The English, and after
it the American, society distinctly stated that the
form of active help which they could give to the
Russian liberation movement would be to win over
to its side, by means of free agitation, the public
opinion, first of their own country, and then of other
free lands. This form of help contains no trace
of license or forced interference in the domestic
affairs of another country, and merely represents
the use of the inalienable right of all men to express
freely what they think and feel.

Here we come to the oft-repeated question : Can
anything so intangible as the expression of what
foreigners think and feel exercise any serious influence over the course of events in Russia ? Can
we expect that a Government which remains deaf
to the demands of public opinion at home will listen
to the voice of foreigners ? Or that the stagnant

waters of Russian patience will be stirred, even to a perceptible ripple, by any storm raised in far-off lands—nay, on the other side of the globe?

These questions and doubts are quite serious, and deserve our full attention. We will, therefore, try to state as clearly as possible our view of the agitation abroad, its conditions, and the extent of its possible influence.

II.

It is hardly necessary to explain that we fully understand that such influence must, by its very nature, be limited. The Russian question must be solved on Russian soil by Russian efforts. That is as it must and as it should be. Every nation worthy of liberty must win her for itself. But we maintain that, with an active support from Russia, the agitation abroad may become a valuable help in the struggle; that, whereas in Russia every step costs terrible sacrifices, the Russian opposition, by working abroad can, without any sacrifices and with a trifling expenditure of energy, create a force which the Government, in spite of its millions of bayonets, will have to take into account.

At the first glance these hopes may seem, to say the least, exaggerated.

It is quite true that the proposed plan of making

use of the foreign press is something new, unknown in former revolutions. But we must not
forget that during the last forty or fifty years there
have happened in the world many new things which
formerly did not exist, or existed only in the germ.
Moreover, the position of Russia and of the Russian
question abroad is also a quite new one.

The sum of many different general influences,
both intellectual and political, have created, so to
say, a new force : the periodical press, above all the
daily press, the newspaper. At any rate they have
developed it to an astonishing extent, rendering it
the greatest power in the world of to-day. The
sum of other conditions and influences has, as it
were, placed this enormous force at the disposal of
the Russian opposition.

Russia, with her population of over a hundred
millions, increasing at so exceptionally rapid a rate,
has always been, and must continue to be, a state
of the first rank as regards her influence on the
general course of European history. The overthrow
of autocracy and the establishment of a free constitutional government in Russia will be an in-
calculable boon to humanity, for with it is bound
up the question of the deliverance of all Central
Europe from the iron yoke of militarism. The fall
of the autocracy in St. Petersburg will render
superfluous and, therefore, impossible the con-

tinuance of the half-autocracy in Berlin. And all
the international relations, the whole political life
of Europe will be changed when true liberty is
introduced into Germany. On the other hand,
every further year that the Russian autocracy
continues to exist is a source of further anxieties,
dangers, nervous tension and material loss and
expense for the whole western world.

The Russian question is therefore a question of
enormous international importance, and concerns
far more interests than those of the Russian people
alone. This circumstance is of the greatest consequence, as it gives stability and firmness to the
Russian cause abroad. Apart from temporary ex-
citements, apart from the ebb and flow of political
curiosity, all that happens in Russia will always be
a matter of deep interest to thinking persons of all
civilised nations. Sympathy with the Russian
movement will grow, steadily and constantly,
together with the growth of general interest in
politics and social questions.

This international character of the Russian
question also affords us the best answer to one
special accusation. The Russian official press has
long been observing our movement. As usual, it
has accused us of "treason," and has poured upon
us a flood of abuse for leaguing with "the enemies
of Russia."

To the gentlemen in the pay of the Russian Government we have nothing to say. But we respect and appreciate patriotic feeling in so far as it is a manifestation of love to one's own race, not an expression of rapacious instincts towards other races. We would rather see in our friends an exaggerated jealousy towards anything that really concerns the dignity of Russian people, than indifference. And, therefore, to those who are honestly hurt by the interference of foreigners in our domestic quarrels, we answer that modern nations have no longer any "domestic" quarrels, properly so-called. Once we have telegraph wires—those nerves of the collective human body—to instantly spread over everywhere the knowledge of all the wrongs and sorrows of the world, all the world suffers with the griefs and misfortunes of every separate people. Every man, as a man, has the right to war against evil, wherever he find it, in the name of the moral suffering which it causes him; he has the right to defend from that suffering both himself and those near to him.

No one now recognises the pretensions of various domestic tyrants to the right of exercising domestic tyranny on the ground that "a household is a secret, private thing," to use the expression put into their mouth by our great national dramatist. And yet the demand for political non-interference, put forward by those to whom the misery of the nation is advantageous, bears just the same character.

But these considerations may appear too abstract and sentimental for a political pamphlet. We therefore prefer to take our stand upon the palpable and inalienable right of foreigners to fight against the Russian autocracy as against a principle *injurious to themselves*, inimical to liberty, retarding progress *in their own land*.

But we, too, are Europeans. For to be a Russian does not involve counting oneself an Asiatic—at least not necessarily so. General European interests are dear to us for their own sake, irrespective of their possible influence on Russian life. We, together with all the advanced parties in Europe, desire to see realised in European life, as rapidly and with as little hindrance as may be, the great principles brought to light by modern social science. We desire the unhindered development of our common culture.

Thus in the struggle on European soil against Russian Tzarism we can join with Europeans as comrades, on a basis of mutual help, in a cause which we consider a quite general one. As for our Jingoes, indignant—perhaps even sincerely indignant—at such a league, we can afford to treat them with the same complete indifference with which we revolutionists treat the howls of the knights-errant of obscurantism in Russia. The analogy is complete.

We hope the reader will not take the above to mean that we attribute the foreign support of the Russian movement to utilitarian motives and policy. We must not confuse what is really the *lawful sanction*—or rather one sanction—of a movement with its true motive force. The *right* to take part in a particular struggle, the right to sacrifice for it time, money, or greater things, has never yet impelled a single human being to really take part in it, or really to sacrifice anything for its sake. For this we need something deeper and more impulsive ; we need the living sympathy which alone can induce a man to labour for the good of others without any advantage to himself—even, it may be, to his own detriment.

This living sympathy is the cause of the movement in Russia, and just so this is the cause of it in England.

But what should suddenly arouse in English people such sympathy with us ? What miracle ? Why this love for Russian liberty and this unselfish desire to help it ? Have the English not cares and difficulties enough of their own ?

Dropping water wears away a stone. The continual talk about the "historical enmity" to us of "perfidious Albion" has left its trace in the minds even of honest and well-meaning persons; and this of course opens to the partisans of reaction a wide field for hints and insinuations.

To those whose astonishment is sincere we can say that they are beginning to be surprised too late in the day. There was a time when the name of Russia was really an object of hatred, in England and throughout Europe; when it was identified with the idea of strangled Poland and Hungary, of a sullen brute force upholding everything reactionary and inhuman in the rest of Europe. But that time is irrevocably past; there now remain but few who confuse the Russian people with the Russian Government. Russia has ceased to be "The Gendarme of Europe"; she has become the land of Siberian exiles, the land of tyranny and of the hopeless misery of the masses; she has become the true Russia which we have known and over which we have mourned.

This change of feeling has come about gradually during the last fifteen or twenty years. The way was prepared by a number of serious investigations which acquainted the scientific and literary world with the Russian people and with Russian culture. But the principal forces at work in the accomplishment of this decided transformation were undoubtedly the Russian novel on the one hand and the Russian revolutionary movement on

6

the other: the poetry of form and the poetry of action; the fascination of the genius of creation and of the genius of self-sacrifice.

The immense success of the Russian novel abroad is known to all educated people. It is a fact not only of literary importance, but of the gravest political significance; it marks an epoch for the Russian cause abroad. Our great novelists have been the propagandists of the Russian idea; they have been the first to convince other nations that the Russian people is not a horde of barbarians, but a great and civilised nation, with boundless potentialities of future development. Reflecting, with the completeness and universality of genius, all sides of Russian life, they have opened to foreigners a whole new world, amazing in its depth and enchanting in its wealth and variety; they first have shown to outsiders the real Russia which had lain hidden behind a forest of bayonets. And there is now no corner of the earth to which the Russian novel has not penetrated, or where it has not won for the Russian people friends and possible partisans of liberty.

The Russian revolutionary movement also has been a revelation to foreigners, as a proof of a political crisis and internal struggle, the existence of which they had not suspected. It showed them the Russians in a new light; it attracted their attention by the energy and dramatic force of the unequal conflict; it conquered their hearts by the irresistible force of sacrifice. This self-abnegation disarms enmity and transforms reproaches and accusations into wondering inquiry already only one step removed from sympathy. The Russian movement, though not understood, has become a living *epos* of our time, winning over to its side public opinion, and awakening alike amazement and sympathy.

America and England read with horror Kennan's mournful narrative, which has left an indelible trace on the mind of the whole contemporary world. Kennan's great work has, once and for all, dispelled the prejudices and misunderstandings concerning our movement, and has placed its aims, motives, and significance in their true light.

These are the sources of the Russian sympathies of foreigners. At the present time there are, among our " historical enemies " the English, just as among our " transatlantic friends," thousands of persons who have become true friends to the real Russia, the Russia of the people. They know and appreciate Russian literature ; they understand the Russian race, know of its troubles, fervently desire its well-being, and believe in its future. We have even, to our astonishment, met with persons who look to Russia for the "new world."

Such persons are, of course, exceptional natures, peculiarly impressionable and responsive to the afflictions of others. They are rare in any one spot; but, counted together, their name is legion; and all these are potential workers for the Russian cause abroad.

With the mass of the reading public the interest in Russia is, of course, superficial. This could not be otherwise, considering the intensity of life in Europe and the press of burning home-questions. But the interest undoubtedly exists, and, being spread over so wide a field, forms an enormous total strength, capable of being utilised for practical work.

Several years ago, reading the biography of Carlo Cattaneo, the hero of the Milan revolution of 1848 and one of the profoundest thinkers of his time, we came upon the following singular fact. Cattaneo, who was not only a *savant* but a brilliant journalist, and who realised the value of foreign public opinion, wished to insert in *The Times* a series of articles. They were intended to acquaint the English public with the state of affairs in Italy, and with the problems before the Italian revolutionists, whom the average Englishman of that day pictured to himself as monsters of much the same kind as the later popular image of the "nihilist." But notwithstanding all the efforts of his English friends, Cattaneo succeeded in getting inserted only one article; the other two he was obliged to publish himself in pamphlet form.

The sympathy of the leaders of. public opinion and the interest in everything Russian, shown by the mass of the reading public, have opened to the Russian cause not only the columns of *The Times*, but also those of the leading papers of all countries, with the exception of France, who still amuses herself with her toy, the "Russian Alliance."

But we make hardly any use of this power. The amount of information that comes from Russia is so small that only an infinitesimal part of the demand can be supplied at first-hand and from authentic sources. But once there is a demand it must be satisfied; and therefore the foreign papers are crowded with all kinds of nonsense about Russia; often with pure inventions, refuted the following day. This only puzzles the public, and casts a shadow of doubt even on authentic news. It is difficult for foreigners to disentangle this mass of statements, and find out where is truth and where falsehood.

A public opinion formed under such conditions cannot have due weight; and the force of the educated world's indignation and sympathy is, as it were, lost in a bog.

The special aim of the " Society of Friends of

Russian Freedom," is to alter this condition of affairs and to utilise in appropriate ways the force given by the sympathy both of that minority for whom the Russian cause is no longer a foreign cause and of the general mass of educated society.

As a means towards the solving of this double problem the society issues a newspaper, as yet of small size, in the English language, in London and New York simultaneously. Of this paper, *Free Russia*, we wish to speak more in detail. It has existed for three and a half years and has now its own circle of five or six thousand readers, the number of which still increases. Notwithstanding the shortness of the period that it has existed, it has won for itself a certain position among the varied mass of periodicals, as the leading organ for Russian affairs. Its voice is beginning to be listened to both in England and on the Continent. This is very much for such a paper, but very little for the Russian cause. So far, the organ has only an educative value. It unites in practical work the friends of Russian freedom who are scattered everywhere; it maintains in a certain circle interest in the Russian cause, and explains by current examples the character and significance of the Russian political crisis. All this prepares the soil; the real work; the real fight will begin only when the paper be-

comes a weapon for widespread and continual influence on the great papers which are read not by
thousands but by millions.

The Russian autocracy cannot exist without the
support of Western Europe; it is in constant need
of money to fill up the holes in its budget; it needs
alliances or friendly neutrality in order that its
showy external politics may distract attention from
the festering sores of its internal politics. In Europe
public opinion rules everything, from the Exchange
to Parliaments and Cabinets; and the press rules
public opinion. For the Russian Government to
maintain as far as possible in the European press
a friendly feeling towards itself is not a sentimental
desire but a matter of state necessity. And, indeed,
notwithstanding its affectation of Olympian serenity,
the Russian Government furtively tries to paralyse,
by fair means or foul, all propaganda hostile to
itself. It hires special literary agents, and, though
needing every farthing of its resources, maintains
foreign papers and bribes everything that is venal in
the European press. When one of the English
"smart journalists," then editor of the Russophile
Pall Mall Gazette, went to St. Petersburg, he was
received with almost official honours. The doors
of the Winter Palace were opened wide for him, and
the Tzar himself favoured the clever journalist with
a long personal audience which many a high Russian

official, wishing to speak on matters of national importance, might have begged for in vain.

If this is Olympian serenity, what is currying favour?

By winning over public opinion to the side of Russian freedom and the Russian people, and thus rendering it hostile to the Russian Government, we can strike the latter a direct, positive, and effectual blow. We have already struck one such blow by undermining at its very foundations the sympathy of the only sincere and trustworthy allies whom the Russian Government had in Europe, the English Liberals, who have now become our principal partisans. We can do more by extending our agitation to the Continent.

There is one question over which the Russian Government has shown an extraordinary sensitiveness and an excitability which verges on the absurd. We refer to the extradition of political offenders. Hundreds of thousands, if not millions, of roubles have been made ducks and drakes of to buy over officials, judges, and ministers in France, Switzerland, and Germany; state interests have been recklessly sacrificed for the sake of extradition treaties; so vehemently does the Government long to put its claws upon some two or three extra "nihilists," and have a chance to boast before the Russian people of the solidarity and support of its great western neighbours.

Thanks to the agitation on English soil, and to it alone, not one lackey now dares to suggest such a treaty with England. In America our position is almost as strong as in this country. The attempt of the Russian Government to openly obtain an extradition treaty in 1886 has been ignominiously defeated by a little stirring up of American public opinion. The friends of the Russian Government dared not so much as to bring the matter before the Senate, and the project was quietly withdrawn by them.

Any open attempt of this kind would have met with the same fate if it had been open to public discussion, be it only for a few weeks. The Russian minister in Washington and his partisans in the legislature knew that, and they resorted to an actual conspiracy in order to palm off upon the unprepared Senate a treaty which they would have repudiated if they had time to learn what it actually meant. The effect of the ratification of the treaty was not entirely harmful : the indignation it has called forth infused new life to our movement in the United States, and it gave Russia's true friends a practical object for their agitation. But the trick would not have succeeded at all if our agitation had spread in the United States not only in breadth but in depth as in England, and the American legislature had among its members men like Mr. Allanson

Picton, Mr. Byles, Mr. Chalmers Morton, and others, who need no explanation to understand and bring home to their colleagues the bearing of any such project.

We have not been able to prevent the ratification of extradition treaties with Germany, Austria, and Switzerland. Our strength in these countries is not sufficient to produce any noticeable effect upon the public opinion.

But we are convinced that when once we can obtain a firm foothold in those countries, we shall be able to annul the treaties and turn the temporary delight and triumph of the Russian Government into shame and disappointment.

We can put more than one spoke into the wheel of our rulers if we trust at once in public opinion and in organised groups of persons of influence in the political, legal, and financial spheres of each separate country.

III.

But long before the Russian movement abroad can become an international political force, it will become a moral force of real influence on both sides of the Russian frontier.

We render full justice to the stupidity and deafness of our rulers. But we must avoid exaggerating

anything, even the obscurantism of Russian Governmental circles. The Government has remained—
and can afford to remain—indifferent to mere dis-
approval, based on general ideas and considerations,
or on facts of doubtful authenticity; but towards
such things as the exposing of the Yakutsk massacre
and the Kara brutalities it could not take up an
attitude of indifference. It ordered an investigation,
it tried to justify itself through the mouths of its
higher officials.

And yet there are committed in Russia every day
—we might almost say every hour—outrages upon
human rights and persons as monstrous as the
Yakutsk massacre or the Kara tragedy. They may
be less sensational, but they are as horrible, if only
because their victims are not units, but thousands
of innocent persons. At present all this is hidden
away. But our friends in Russia only need to make
a small effort, and these things could be upon every
tongue.

If one-tenth—nay, one-hundredth—of the shameful
deeds that are committed in Russia in the dark, were
brought to light, day by day, and pilloried before
the whole educated world, neither the Russian
Government nor any other could remain indifferent.
Quite apart from the unconquerable sense of shame
which is felt by even bullies of the purest water when
actions of theirs are exposed which they themselves

cannot deny to be disgraceful, another feeling begins to show itself—the fear of the reflected influence which such exposures must have upon public opinion in Russia itself.

The assiduousness of the French Republic may to some extent paralyse the external results of the agitation abroad ; but its reflection within Russia cannot be paralysed, and will grow with its growth. We hope to follow up, in time, the publication of the English newspaper with editions in several European languages, Russian among the number. George Kennan, to whom belongs the lion's share in the creation of the Russian movement abroad, has already suggested the simultaneous issue in America of *Free Russia* in English and in Russian.

This, in our eyes, is the final aim and meaning of the agitation abroad. With the exception of France, the whole Western world sympathises with the cause of Russian liberation. As to France, we can do without her. The Anglo-Saxon race, England and America—not to speak of the other continental nations—forms a sufficiently broad support for any movement. Among the English and Americans we have thousands of fervent partisans who are willing to express their sympathy, not in words alone. Their only difficulty is to realise how and by what means they can help in a struggle of such peculiar character as that in Russia. To them we say : Help us to show the world a true and, as far as possible, complete picture of what is being done in our time in Russia. Light, if well concentrated and well directed, can traverse enormous distances with a scarcely perceptible diminution of intensity; and what is done in Russia can be clearly seen by a light thrown from London or New York. Let us, then, unite our efforts to throw this light upon Russia; for if we can do that, sympathy from abroad will, to some extent, replace the publicity that is forbidden within the land.

We, as Russians, have a right to invite foreigners to join in this irreproachable work. Foreigners have undertaken and will continue it, as it is fully in harmony with the spirit, customs, and ideas of free peoples.

Our paper receives material help and expressions of sympathy from all parts of the earth, even from such far-off corners as South Africa, New Zealand, and the Malay Archipelago. In England and America there have gathered round the paper groups of friends, who, for determination, stedfastness, and serious attitude towards their work, might serve as an example to many Russian organisations. The support given to the movement already begun may increase to an *unlimited extent* if only the mass of sympathisers can see tangible proof that the work which they have undertaken is really serious, that

their agitation may really become an actual power,
that it does truly, to some extent, take the place of
the right of publicity in Russia. Nothing but active
support from Russia can convince them of this.

IV.

We appeal to all opponents of the Russian autocracy without distinction of party—to socialists
and Liberals alike. Our work stands outside of
all parties ; it is devoted solely to the interests of
Russian political freedom, which all Russian parties
agree in desiring.

Everything that affects the fate of Russia depends
upon what is done in Russia by Russians. The
work abroad is no exception to this rule. Nay, we
may even say that the efficacy—the very possibility
—of the movement abroad depends upon the existence of an active protest in Russia. Who is
interested in the question of, say, Turkish or Persian
liberty, when the Turks and Persians in no way
show themselves discontented ? An agitation abroad
can grow and develop only if there is a parallel
movement on Russian soil. The present foreign
movement is nothing more than a reflection of the
struggle which existed in Russia in the seventies and
in the beginning of the eighties. The best help that

our Russian comrades can now give to the foreign movement is to take part in the struggle which is coming into life in Russia.

The beginning of the nineties promises to open a new epoch for the Russian revolutionary movement. In face of the utter incapacity of the Government to cope with the terrible misfortune which it has brought upon the land, the discontent in Russia is becoming wider and keener, and is spreading to spheres of society which up till now have been mere ballast in politics. The villages are already in a state of disturbance. But one need not be a prophet to foresee that there will soon be far greater disturbance in the towns, where the conscious opposition is concentrated, and to which the irritated, starving crowds are flocking. Under such conditions the discontent must inevitably find active expression in one form or another; and, we hope, in a wider form than it has taken up till now. The fate of Russia depends, to a great extent, upon what takes place during the next two or three years. But, just because of the enormous importance of the moment, it would be an unpardonable blunder not to employ in the interests of the Russian movement an instrument of such large effect upon the consciousness of society as the free foreign press. The foreign press must complete and uphold our work ; it must increase the weight of every blow, thus rendering the victory easier and shortening the trying period of struggle. And we must remember that every month, every week of the fight costs Russia hundreds of victims, ruins thousands of lives which might be preserved for a better future.

LETTER SENT BY THE REVOLUTIONARY EXECUTIVE COMMITTEE TO ALEXANDER III. AT HIS ACCESSION TO THE THRONE.

"*March* 10, 1881.

"YOUR MAJESTY, — Although the Executive Committee understands fully the grievous oppression that you must experience at this moment, it believes that it has no right to yield to the feeling of natural delicacy which would perhaps dictate the postponement of the following explanation to another time. There is something higher than the most legitimate human feeling, and that is duty to one's country—the duty for which a citizen must sacrifice himself and his own feelings, and even the feelings of others. In obedience to this all-powerful duty we have decided to address you at once, waiting for nothing, as will wait for nothing the historical process that threatens us with rivers of blood and the most terrible convulsions.

\ " The tragedy enacted on the Ekaterinski Canal [1] was not a mere casualty, nor was it unexpected. After all that had happened in the course of the previous decade it was absolutely inevitable, and in that fact consists its deep significance for a man who has been placed by fate at the head of Governmental authority. Such occurrences can be explained as the results of individual malignity, or even of the evil disposition of 'gangs' only by one who is wholly incapable of analysing the life of a nation. For then whole years, notwithstanding the strictest persecution, notwithstanding the sacrifice by the late Emperor's Government of liberty, even its own dignity ; notwithstanding the absolute sacrifice of everything in the attempt to suppress the revolutionary movement, that movement has obstinately extended, attracting to itself the best elements of the country, the most energetic and self-sacrificing people of Russia, and the revolutionists have carried on for three years a desperate warfare with the administration.

"You are aware, your Majesty, that the government of the late Government could not be accused of a lack of energy. It hanged the innocent and guilty and filled prisons and remote provinces with exiles. Tens of so-called ' leaders ' were captured and hanged, and died with the courage and

[1] The place where Alexander II. was killed.

tranquillity of martyrs; but the movement did not
cease—on the contrary, it grew and strengthened.
The revolutionary movement, your Majesty, is not
dependent upon any particular individuals. It is a
process of the social organism, and the scaffolds
raised for its more energetic exponents are as
powerless to save the outgrown order of things as
the cross that was erected for the Redeemer was
powerless to save the ancient world from the triumph
of Christianity. The Government, of course, may
yet capture and harry an immense number of individuals, it may break up a great number of separate
revolutionary groups, it may even destroy the most
important of existing revolutionary organisations;
but all this will not change in the slightest degree
the condition of affairs. Revolutionists are the
creation of circumstances of the general discontent
of the people—of the striving of Russia after a new
social framework. It is impossible to exterminate
a whole people—it is impossible, by means of repression, to stifle its discontent. Discontent only
grows the more when it is repressed. For this
reason the places of slain revolutionists are constantly taken by new individuals, who come forth
from among the people in ever-increasing numbers,
and who are still more embittered, still more energetic. These persons, in order to carry on the
conflict, form an association in the light of the

experience of their predecessors, and the revolutionary organisation thus grows stronger numerically and in quality with the lapse of time. This we actually see from the history of the last ten years. Of what use was it to destroy the Dolgushinzy,[1] the Chaikovzy, and the workers of 1874? Their places were taken by much more resolute democrats. Then the awful repressive measures of the Government called upon the stage the terrorists of 1878 and 1879. In vain the Government put to death the Kovalskys, the Dubrovins, the Ossinskys, and the Lisogubs. In vain it destroyed dozens of revolutionary circles. From among those incomplete organisations, by virtue of natural selection, arose only stronger forms, until at last there has appeared an Executive Committee, with which the Government has not yet been able successfully to deal.

" A dispassionate glance at the grievous decade through which we have just passed will enable us to forecast accurately the future progress of the revolutionary movement, provided the policy of the Government does not change. The movement will continue to grow and extend, deeds of terrorist nature will increase in frequency and intensity, and the revolutionary organisation will constantly

---

[1] The famous groups of so-called propagandists, who virtually began the modern revolutionary struggle.

set forth in the places of destroyed groups stronger
and more perfect forms. Meanwhile the number of
the discontented in the country will grow larger and
larger; confidence in the Government on the part of
the people will decline, and the idea of revolution,
of its possibility and inevitability, will establish
itself in Russia more and more firmly. A terrible
explosion, a bloody hurly-burly, a revolutionary
earthquake throughout Russia will complete the
destruction of the old order of things. Upon
what depends this terrible prospect ? Yes, your
Majesty, 'terrible and lamentable'! Do not take
this for a mere phrase. We understand better than
any one else can how lamentable is the waste of so
much talent and energy, the loss in bloody skir-
mishes, and in the work of destruction of so much
strength, that under other conditions might have
been expended in creative labour and in the development of the intelligence, the welfare, and civil life
of the Russian people. Whence proceeds this
lamentable necessity for bloody conflict ? It arises,
your Majesty, from the lack in Russia of a real
Government in the true sense of that word. A
Government, in the very nature of things, should
only give outward form to the aspirations of the
people and effect to the people's will. But with us
—excuse the expression—the Government has de-
generated into a mere camarilla, and deserves the

name of a 'usurping gang' much more than does
the Executive Committee.

"Whatever may be the *intentions* of the Tzar, the
actions of the Government have nothing in common
with the popular welfare or the popular aspirations.
The Imperial Government subjected the people to
serfdom, put the masses into the power of the
nobility, and is now openly creating the most injurious class of speculators and jobbers. All of its
reforms result merely in a more perfect enslavement
and a more complete exploiting of the people. It
has brought Russia to such a pass that at the
present time the masses of the people are in a state
of pauperism and ruin, are subjected to the most
humiliating surveillance, even at their own domestic
hearths, and are powerless to regulate their own
communal and social affairs. The protection of the
law and of the Government is enjoyed only by the
extortionists and the exploiters, and the most ex-
asperating robbery goes unpunished. But, on the
other hand, what a terrible fate awaits the man who
seriously considers the general good! You know
very well, your Majesty, that it is not only socialists who are exiled and prosecuted. Can it be
possible that the *Government* is the guardian of such
'order'? Is it not rather probable that this is
the work of a 'gang,' the evidence of a complete
usurpation?

" These are the reasons why the Russian Government exerts no moral influence and has no support among the people. These are the reasons why Russia brings forth so many revolutionists. These are the reasons why even such a deed as Tzaricide excites in the minds of a majority of the people only gladness and sympathy. Yes, your Majesty! do not be deceived by the reports of flatterers and sycophants—Tzaricide in Russia is popular.

" From such a state of affairs there can be only two exits : either a revolution, absolutely inevitable and not to be averted by any punishments, or a voluntary turning of the Supreme Power to the people. In the interest of our native land, in the hope of preventing the useless waste of energy, in the hope of averting the terrible miseries that always accompany revolution, the Executive Committee approaches your Majesty with the advice to take the second course. Be assured, so soon as the Supreme Power ceases to rule arbitrarily, so soon as it firmly resolves to accede to the demands of the people's conscience and consciousness, you may, without fear, discharge the spies that disgrace the administration, send your guards back to their barracks, and burn the scaffolds that are demoralising the people. The Executive Committee will voluntarily terminate its own existence, and the organisations formed about it will disperse, in order that their members may devote themselves to the work of culture among the people of their native land.

"We address your Majesty as those who have discarded all prejudices and who have suppressed the distrust created by the actions of the Government throughout the century. We forget that you are the representative of the authority that has so often deceived and that has so injured the people. We address you as a citizen and as an honest man. We hope that the feeling of personal exasperation will not extinguish in your mind your consciousness of your duties and your desire to know the truth. *We* also might feel exasperation. You have lost your father. We have lost not only our fathers, but our brothers, our wives, our children, and our dearest friends. But we are ready to suppress personal feeling, if it be demanded by the welfare of Russia. We expect the same from you.

"We set no conditions for you; do not let our propositions irritate you. The conditions that are pre-requisite to a change from revolutionary activity to peaceful labour are created not by us, but by history. These conditions in our opinion are two:—

"1. A general amnesty to cover all past political crimes; for the reason that they were not crimes, but fulfilments of civil duties.

" 2. The summoning of representatives of the whole Russian people to examine the existing framework of social and Governmental life, and to remodel it in accordance with the people's wishes.

" We regard it as necessary, however, to remind you that the legalisation of the Supreme Power by the representatives of the people, can be valid only in case the elections are perfectly free. For this reason such elections must be held under the following conditions :—

" 1. Delegates are to be sent from all classes without distinction, and in number are to be proportionate to the number of inhabitants.

" 2. There shall be no limitations either for voters or delegates.

" 3. The canvass and the elections shall be absolutely unrestricted, and therefore the Government, pending the organisation of the National Assembly, shall authorise, in the form of temporary measures—

" (a) Complete freedom of the press.

" (b) Complete freedom of speech.

" (c) Complete freedom of public meeting.

" (d) Complete freedom of election programmes.

" This is the only way in which Russia can return to the path of normal and peaceful development.

" We declare solemnly, before the people of our

native land and before the whole world, that our
party will submit unconditionally to the decisions
of a National Assembly elected in the manner
above indicated, and that we will not allow ourselves in the future to offer violent resistance to
any Government that the National Assembly may
sanction.

"And now, your Majesty, decide! Before you
are two courses, and you are to make your choice
between them. We can only trust that your
intelligence and conscience may suggest to you
the only decision that is compatible with the
welfare of Russia, with your own dignity, and
with your duty to your native land.

"THE EXECUTIVE COMMITTEE."

THE LIBERAL PROGRAMME.

*From the Liberals of Moscow to Count Loris Melikoff,
Chief of the Supreme Executive Commission.*

Now let us draw the reader's attention to another
document, coming from quite a different source, yet
which, making allowance for the tone, resembles the
former one not only in the final conclusions, but in the
general ideas and views upon the conditions of the
country, the appreciations of the evils from which it
is suffering, and of the possible remedies, at times
repeating almost the same expressions. This
document is a letter or memorandum to the Tzar ,
from a representative body of men, who may be
fairly called the Liberal Executive. It refers to the
same period as the letter of the Revolutionary
Executive we have just quoted, that is to say to
the period of the most fierce struggle between the
terrorists and the autocracy. After having vainly
tried the policy of reprisals, the Tzar Alexander II.
appointed the " Liberal " Loris Melikoff to the post
of virtual dictator. The moderate section of the
opposition—the Liberals—resolved to try once again ,
the effect of peaceful exhortations. Twenty-five of

them, who were the most courageous and influential
in their party, including professors of the universities, leading barristers, well-known authors, and
representative and able citizens of the old capital,
drew up a memorandum which they all signed, and
which one of them carried personally to Loris
Melikoff in March, 1880, with the request to lay it
before the Tzar.

This interesting document, the publication of
which we owe to the indefatigable zeal of Mr.
George Kennan, throws a flood of light upon the
attitude and views of the actual, though not officially
recognised, representatives of the country.

I will quote here its most characteristic passages,
putting in parenthesis a few occasional words to
make its meaning clearer to English readers.

" The unfortunate conditions of Russia at the
present time," so runs the memorandum, " is due to
the fact that there has arisen in Russian society a
party [the terrorists] which acts with great irration-
ality, and is carrying on a contest with the Government in a manner with which right-thinking people,
no matter what their position or degree of education, cannot sympathise. This contest, which is
seditious in its character, manifests itself in a series
of acts of violence directed against the ruling
authorities. The question is, how can the evil be
remedied ?

" In order to answer this question it is necessary first to uncover the real causes of the evil. The object of the present letter is to show :

" *First.* That the principal reason for the morbid form which the contest with the Government has taken is the absence in Russia of any opportunity for the free development of public opinion and the free exercise of public activity.

" *Second.* That the evil cannot be eradicated by any sort of repressive measures.

" *Third.* That the present condition of the people, many of whose most urgent needs are wholly unsatisfied, constitutes ample causes for dissatisfaction, and that this dissatisfaction, having no means of free expression, necessarily manifests itself in morbid forms.

" *Fourth.* That the causes which underlie this widespread discontent cannot be removed by Governmental action alone, but require the friendly co-operation of all the vital forces of society.

" The unnatural form which the contest with the Government has taken is due to the absence of all means for the free and orderly expression of public discontent. Dissatisfaction cannot be expressed through the press, since the press is closely restricted in its comments upon Governmental action. Questions of first-class importance are wholly removed by censorial prohibition from the field of newspaper discussion, and that at the very time when they most occupy public attention. Newspapers are not even allowed to publish facts, if such facts compromise or reflect in any way upon Governmental organs.

"Another reason for the development of ' underground' activity may be found in the enforced silence of public assemblies. The Government often treats with contemptuous neglect statemer..s and petitions from sources fully competent to make them, and listens unwillingly to the representatives even of the most legitimate interests. There may be found in the reports of any provincial administration records of innumerable petitions sent by the assemblies to the Government, which not only have never been granted, but have never been even answered.

"The result of the state of things above set forth is the creation of an impression the Government does not wish to listen to the voice of the people; that it will not tolerate criticism, however just, of its mistakes and failures; that it despises the opinions of competent advisers, and that it has in view peculiar objects not related in any way to the necessities of the people. [This means the same as pp. 86 of the former letter.]

"The impossibility of speaking out frankly compels people to keep their ideas to themselves, to cherish and nurse them in secret, and to regard complacently even illegal methods of putting them into practice [this means terrorism, revolution, &c.]. Thus is created one of the most important of the conditions upon which the spread of sedition depends, namely, the weakening of the loyalty of those who, under other circumstances, would regard sedition with abhorrence.

"There are in organised societies self-reliant opinions, which strike for free expression, an accumulated fund of energy, which seeks a field for activity. The more rigorously these impulses are repressed in their legal form the sooner they will take on a form which is not legal; the more apparent will become the lack of harmony between the strivings of society and the working methods of the ruling powers; and the more general and emphatic and consequently the more infectious will become the illegal protest. When society has no means of ʓ making known and discussing peaceably and publicly its wants and its necessities, the more energetic members of that society will throw themselves passionately into secret activity [*i.e.* terrorism, Revolution].

"At the present time there is a prevalent opinion that the existing evils can be eradicated only by repressive measures. Many people believe that before anything else is thought of, attention should be concentrated upon methods of repression, and that when such methods shall have attained the result expected from them, it will be time enough to proceed with the further development of Russian social life. But the evils cannot be remedied by repressive measures; and that is not all—repressive measures not only do not cure the evils which exist, but they create new evils, because they are inevitably accompanied by administrative license. License above creates license below.

"But aside from all this, repression cannot kill human thought. Convincing proof of this fact is furnished by the last reign (Nicholas I.) as well as by more recent years. The idea of popular representation, for example, has recently taken enormous strides forward and has made its way even into the far distant country places, notwithstanding the fact that public discussion or consideration of that idea has been absolutely forbidden.

"In the absence of a free press there arises another medium of inter-communication in the shape of the oral transmission of ideas from mouth to mouth.

"The most marked feature of the present situation in Russia is extreme dissatisfaction and urgent need of free expression. Educated society as a whole, irrespective of rank, position, or opinions, is intensely dissatisfied, and out of that dissatisfaction arises the existing agitation.

"The first and most important of society's un-satisfied demands is the demand for an opportunity to act. This demand even a constantly growing bureaucracy has been unable to silence. The old mechanism of Government proved to be incapable of directing the new and complex forces which were in operation. Only by the free and independent efforts of society itself could they be regulated and con-trolled. The striving of the people for an opportunity to act—to take part in the control of the national life [supremacy of national parliament]—has therefore become a phenomenon which the ruling power must take into account. Unfortunately, however, it is a phenomenon which the administrator regards with hostility. At the very moment when society is aroused both by the nature of its own reflections and by the circumstances of the time [revolutionary struggle] and seeks to participate in the life of the State, the administration throws obstacles in its way. If the ruling mechanism in its present form excludes from direct participation in the government a majority of those who have the first right and the strongest desire to take part in it, than that mechanism stands in need of reformation.

"The Russian people are becoming more and more impressed with the conviction that an empire so extensive and a social life so complicated as ours, cannot be managed exclusively by officials.

8

"Another demand of society which at the present time is even less satisfied than the desire for political activity is the demand for personal security. The indispensable conditions upon which the very existence of modern society depends are free courts, freedom from arrest, and search without proper precautions and safeguards, and responsibility of officials for illegal detention and imprisonment, and the due observance of all the legal formalities of public and controversial trial.

"In the almost unlimited province of political crime, where the features which distinguish the permissible from the forbidden are so difficult of definition (according to Russian official views, of course), and where, consequently, personal liberty should be surrounded by the greatest possible safeguards, there exists a state of things which is in flagrant violation of the most elementary principles of justice.

"For the past ten years the police, upon trivial suspicion or upon a false accusation, have been allowed to break into houses, force their way into the sphere of private life, read private letters, throw the accused into prison, keep them there for months, and finally subject them to an inquisitorial examination without even informing them definitely of the nature of the charges made against them. Many persons have been arrested in this way by mistake or under misapprehension.

" Still more out of harmony with the views of the people is the system of administrative exile and banishment without examination or trial. Whilst the spirit of the law and the first principles of justice forbid the infliction of punishment without previous trial, hundreds, and perhaps thousands, of persons annually are subjected to the severest punishment that can be inflicted upon an educated man, namely, banishment from home and friends, and that by a mere administrative order, based upon nothing. Persons exiled in this way have no means of knowing how long their punishment will continue. They are deprived even of the consolation which every common criminal has in knowing definitely the length of time he has to suffer.

" The discontent which pervades Russian society and which is the result of the mistaken policy of the Government in dealing with internal affairs, can be removed only by measures in which society will take part. The Government cannot accomplish the · desired result alone. The only way to extricate the country from its present position is to summon an independent parliament—*Sobranie*—consisting of the representatives of the *Zemstvos ;* to give that parliament a share in the control of the national life, and to securely guarantee personal rights, freedom of thought and freedom of speech. Such freedom will call into action the best capabilities of the people, will rouse the slumbering life of the nation, and will develop the abundant productive resources of the country.

"The Russians are fit for free institutions, and they feel deep humiliation at being kept so long under guardianship. The desire for such institutions, although forced into concealment and half-stifled by repressive measures, finds expression, neverthe-less, in the *Zemstvos*, in the assemblies of the nobles, and in the press. The granting of such institutions and the calling together of a representative body to preside over them, will give to the nation renewed strength and renewed faith in the Government and in its own future."

THE CLAIMS OF THE RUSSIAN
LIBERALS.

THE CLAIMS OF THE RUSSIAN LIBERALS.

WHATEVER has been printed in English about the Russian political movement has been almost exclusively confined to the so-called revolutionists, or "nihilists," as they are often termed in this country—that is, to people who have lost all faith in getting for the Russian people a brighter light and a better day by any other means but violently overthrowing the present *régime*. There was hardly anything except George Kennan's "Last Appeal of the Russian Liberals," printed in the *Century Magazine*, dealing with any attempts to get the same by peaceful and "legal" means. One of the effects of this was that many people got the wrong impression that in the whole mass of the Russian nation there was only a handful of revolutionary spirits who wanted political changes, while all the rest were quite satisfied by the existing *régime*. Of course all the interested and the disinterested supporters of the Russian Government tried to strengthen that impression. They maintained that every one within Russia was contented with the present form of government, the only malcontents and aspirants for political changes being a small set of troublesome people full of perverted ideas and exulting in political crime. Some of these champions of a bad cause went so far as to assert that "the Russian nation urged its Government to take energetic measures against the revolutionists."

In reality there is plenty of evidence to prove the contrary, although every difficulty is put in the way of the Russian people's expressing their wishes freely; the press is gagged, political meetings are strictly prohibited; as to the local councils (*zemstvos*), assemblies of the nobility, town councils (*doumas*), and similar bodies, either the law or administrative practice very carefully and strictly limits their right of petitioning the Government to local or class wants.

Notwithstanding that, however, the nobility and the *zemstvos* (as well as some of the *doumas*) have from time to time profited by the opportunity, when Governmental discipline slackened, of expressing their hidden and intimate aspirations and views which do not show much satisfaction with the present state of things. So far back as the year 1865 the nobility of the Moscow province presented the Tzar Alexander II. with a "most devoted" petition, entreating the monarch "to convene a representative assembly of the people of Russia to discuss the question of the wants common to the whole country." To this the Tzar replied by proclaiming that "no class of the population has the right to speak in the name of other classes, and to take on themselves the initiative in questions of which the solution depends exclusively on the Head of the State." This step of the Tzar was really a breach of the privileges of the nobility, as solemnly acknowledged by the Russian monarchs.

In 1866 the Government restricted the rights of the *zemstvo* to impose rates for local necessities on the wealthiest part of the population. On this occasion Count Andrew Shouvalov, a member of the St. Petersburg *zemstvo*, delivered at its session of 1867 several forcible speeches in which, criticising the new law and its preparation without any participation of the *zemstvos* in it, he proposed to petition the Government that the grave questions raised by that law should be inquired into "by the combined efforts and common work both of the administration and of the whole Russian *zemstvo*." "I say 'of the whole Russian *zemstvo*,'" accentuated the speaker, "because, if discussed separately by different provincial assemblies, the result may come to have the same disadvantage as now; that is, may be as one-sided as now." The St. Petersburg local assembly accepted the Count's proposal. But the Government answered the petition by closing for a time the *zemstvo* institutions of the province altogether, and by administrative exile of some of its members to eastern provinces. Side by side with this, the curtailing of even those very limited rights which were granted to the *zemstvos* when they were instituted was further continued.

In the meantime the revolutionists gathered more and more strength, and gradually became so formidable that on August 4, 1878, the Government inserted in No. 186 of *The Official Messenger* an appeal to the peaceful class of society, asking for help against the "revolutionary plague." In November of the same year Alexander II. delivered a speech in Moscow, in which, addressing the representatives of different classes, he said, "I count on your assistance in stopping the erring youths on that ruinous path into which some untrustworthy people try to lure them." Five local assemblies (Kharkov, Poltava, Chernigov, Samara, and Tver) profited by the opportunity and answered the appeal by presenting the Tzar's Government with memoranda, in which, while manifesting their thorough loyalty, they expressed most explicitly the belief that there was no outlet from the difficulty but in granting personal security to citizens, political liberty, and representative government. Only the Kharkov memorandum reached officially its destination, being presented by the governor of the province, through the ministry to the Tzar, and the consequence was that the discussion of the subject was declared by the Government to transgress the powers and aims of the *zemstvos;* all further transactions on the matter were prohibited, and the governors of the other four provinces, acting on instructions from St. Petersburg, declined to accept the further memoranda for presentation, at the same time forbidding them to be made public. In fact, besides the Kharkov memorandum, only two others (those of Tver and Chernigov) ever appeared in print, and that *despite* the Governmental *veto.* These documents are quite sufficient, however, to show clearly the views and claims of the peaceful and loyal part of the Russian Liberals of that time.

The Chernigov *zemstvo* not only does not urge the Government to use coercion and terrorism against the revolutionists, but declines to take any part in it itself. "The late events have shown it clearly," so runs the memorandum, "that penal and coercive measures are powerless to stop the flood of subversive ideas. . . . And if punishment, which, according to our ' code,' is more severe than in any other European legislation, proves to be impotent to abash the erring ones, this points to the existence of causes which are unavoidable and in which originate the lamentable facts." . . . Of these causes three are, in the estimation of the *zemstvo*, the most important (besides some others of minor importance), namely :—

" 1. The present organisation of (Governmental) middle and higher class schools.

" 2. The lack of freedom of speech and the press.

" 3. The lack of respect to law in our society."

Then, after showing that all the three evils were created and maintained by the policy and unlawful practices of the Government itself, the memorandum concluded as follows : "Under the circumstances the provincial *zemstvo* of Chernigov states with a most unexpressible heavy heart that it is powerless to take any practical steps in the struggle with the evil, and considers it its duty to bring this to the knowledge of the Government."

The starting-point of the Tver memorandum was the same as that of Chernigov. It proceeded with a very definite charge against the Ministry of National Education. That Ministry, it is said, while preventing the *zemstvo* from taking any part in the direction of schools (which are in Russia *all* either in the hands or under the strictest control of the Government), manages the middle schools in such a way that one-eighth of the whole number of pupils leave them before completing their studies. As to those who enter the universities and similar institutions, "suspicion and coercion await them, which make quiet study impossible, while calling forth discontent and irritation, conditions under which respect of law is hardly to be expected to be developed in our youths."

Disrespect to law is further cultivated by the Government among grown-up citizens. " His Imperial Majesty has granted to the Russian people the *zemstvo*-self-government in which we cannot fail seeing the pledge of a peaceful and lawful national development. We are grieved to say, however, that the administration restricted the *zemstvo's* activity, and really deprived it of any real importance ; even its most modest petitions on account of its dire needs remain unsatisfied, nay, unanswered. An independent, fair, prompt, and humane administration of justice is indispensable to secure to life its regular course, and to sustain the idea of the sacredness of law in the minds of the people—an idea without which no state can exist. Such a judiciary was granted us by his Majesty on the 20th of November, 1864. But the administrative practice of the Government undermines the sacredness of justice; confidence in law, as maintained by inviolable decisions of the courts, is shaken ; the court and the law cease to safeguard the citizen, who becomes exposed to the good or ill will of an arbitrary administration. All this is only preparing the soil for subversive ideas. Subversive ideas might find a formidable enemy in the press ; but the press, as is well known, is also deprived of any possibility to treat social questions independently, and while the number of clandestine publications grows, the organs of the press are compelled to stop one after the other."

The memorandum of the Tver *zemstvo* concluded by stating that the Russian people felt it impossible to do anything against the internal evil unless the Government would remove the above-mentioned social conditions which originate that evil, and which it is altogether within the power of the Government to remove. "His Imperial Majesty, with kind care for the welfare of the Bulgarian people, just liberated from the Turkish yoke, thought it indispensable to grant to that people a true self-government, personal security, independence of the judges, and liberty of the press. The *zemstvo* of the Tver province dares to hope that the Russian people, who bore all the burdens of the war with such a thorough readiness, with such love towards its Tzar, the liberator, will be allowed to enjoy the same blessings which alone can enable it to enter, in virtue of our monarch's will, the path of gradual, peaceful, and lawful development."

It will be easily understood that the injustice, arbitrariness, and insincerity with which Alexander II. and his Government treated the Russian Liberals strengthened the position of the revolutionists. The latter proclaimed the Government hopeless, a Government that could not be trusted; and the manner in which the peaceful and loyal class of society was treated, that very class to which it applied itself in difficulty, justified the uncompromising attitude of the revolutionary party in the eyes of many who before thought differently. Among other reasons, we find here the explanation of the enormous activity the revolutionary party developed, notwithstanding the comparatively small number of its acknowledged adherents—an activity which culminated in the death of Alexander II.

That tragedy raised again a burning question for the peaceful citizens of Russia who cared for the welfare of the community. They wanted to put an end to the deplorable internal struggle, they wanted to remain loyal to the Tzar and to do their duty as citizens; but they felt that neither was possible so long as the Government clung obstinately to bureaucratism and autocracy and suppressed aspirations towards liberty and self-government. At the same time they had no earnest trust of the Government's good faith or grasp of the political situation. That is evident from speeches that were delivered in some of the *zemstvo*-assemblies, convened soon after the 13th of March, 1881.

In the Novgorod *zemstvo* one of its members, N. N. Nechayev, delivered a speech in which, among other things, he said: " Hardly can we doubt that it is our duty to speak out on this occasion. True, the literal meaning of the '*zemstvo* statutes' does not grant us that right. But it is impossible to be guided only by the literal meaning of the law at a moment of such historical importance as the present ; we have to elevate ourselves and to see what is the spirit of the law. According to the 'statutes' we are empowered to deal only with *local* interests. But it is impossible to separate the welfare of the Tzar from any local interests ! Is not his welfare the most urgent interest of any locality and any person ? The historical moment we are living through is a horrible one ! Look around you, account to yourself for what is going on, and you will find it impossible to be silent.

"We have before our eyes a long series of endeavours to fight the evil purely by means of police measures, without any co-operation with society. The utter uselessness of such a struggle and the impossibility of obtaining any real success on that path is nowadays evident to every one. There is no going further on that path ; it is also impossible to listen to appeals to reaction, as that would mean renouncing the great principles which were bequeathed to us by the late monarch. So only one path remains open : society must be called upon to take part in the struggle with the evil, *then* there can be no doubt about the issue."

The Samara *zemstvo* was still more explicit and far less hopeful.

On March 18, 1881, its president[1] proposed to present Alexander III. with an address, in which the feelings of grief at the sad end of the late Tzar, as well as congratulations on his own accession to the throne, were expressed. But the deputy, Zhdanov, opposed the motion. "During the last few years," he said, "we have presented five similar addresses; none of them led to anything, nor did they really express anything, *because all that was in fact weighing on our souls was unrevealed and still remains so.*" He was supported by two other speakers. The deputy Näoumov said, "We do not know what awaits us.[2] It is better, therefore, to keep silence." The deputy Noudatov said he now considered it a question whether he was right in signing the preceding addresses. "Did we ever mention in them the over-burdening of the peasantry with taxes, the crushing of labour by capital, the lack of safeguards to personal liberty? No; we never did! Well, then, it is better not to say anything at all—to be silent."

[The motion of the president was declined almost unanimously.]

---

[1] The presidents of the *zemstvo* assemblies are, according to law, the marshals of the local nobility, which is often not in accordance with the wishes of the assemblies.

[2] That is, what the attitude of the central Government towards the *zemstvo* will be.—F. V.

We are unable to mention here all the *zemstvos*
that at that time expressed themselves in favour of
representative government and political liberty, as
the publication of the accounts of the sessions were
dependent upon the permission of the governor of
the province. We know, however, that the *zemstvos*
of Ryazan, Taurida, and Kazan, also the *douma* of
Kazan and the nobility of Samara were among them.

Loris Melikov was succeeded in his capacity as
Minister of Internal Affairs by Count Ignatïev. On
May 6, 1881, the new minister published a circular,
in which he again appealed to society at large for
help against the revolutionists, and in establishing
order and peace in the empire. And again he
received from many *zemstvos* the same reply : " We
are powerless to do anything so long as we are
exposed to the arbitrary and lawless practices of
the administration ; we are unable to help the
Government unless it establishes a central body of
representatives from the *zemstvos*."

Then Count Ignatïev convened a " commission of
experts " chosen *by the Government* from the midst of
the *zemstvos*, as well as from people who did not
belong to them. He wanted to satisfy the Liberals
with a mummy of representative government. But
the Liberals would not be satisfied. In the next
session of the Novgorod provincial assembly, for
example, deputy E. I. Ragozin said that the

members of the said commission "cannot be regarded as representing the *zemstvos;* that is only a fictitious representation, and in discussing the gravest questions which concern the *zemstvos* as well as the whole nation, the commission only creates misunderstanding among the population, because the opinions expressed in it are taken as being those of deputies elected by the people, while in reality the members of that body are chosen by the Ministry of Internal Affairs."

We have quoted sufficiently from the different speeches delivered in the assemblies of nobles or assemblies for local affairs, and also from the memorandums and resolutions passed by them. It is evident from these quotations, that that part of the Russian people, which holds in its hands the landed property of the empire, and to a large extent the different branches of manufacture and trade, look with great dissatisfaction upon the present arbitrary Russian rule, feel deeply its outrages upon the population, and ask, whenever they can, for a *habeas corpus,* political liberty and representative government. So far as has transpired, at different times seventeen *zemstvos* in all, also two *doumas* (town councils), and the nobility of three provinces have made such declarations. Besides that, the Mayor of Moscow expressed similar wishes at a public banquet, which was the more significant, in that the speech was made at the coronation of the present Tzar, in the elder capital of the empire, which has always been considered the most loyal, and the mayor himself was a late professor of the Moscow University. But we are sure that these were not by any means all the bodies who have, though in courteous and loyal terms, condemned the present Governmental system in Russia, and asked for liberty and constitutional government.

Now what was the attitude of the Tzar and his Government towards those just aspirations of his loyal and peaceful subjects? Foreseeing them, the *zemstvos* had not been given the right of electing the chairmen of their assemblies. The marshals of the nobility had been appointed as such, and made responsible for everything said by the deputies on the one hand, and on the other given the power of stopping any discussion. No report of the debates or declaration of any *zemstvo* can be printed without a special permit of the governor of the province. And if we look at the records of the proceedings of the local boards, we shall see that the *vetos* either of the chairmen or of the governors intervened nearly every time, when the questions discussed touched the vital points of national life. When, however, the Russian people contrived to make themselves heard notwithstanding all this gagging, then the Tzar in person showed his displeasure and declined to grant his people a fair hearing. Imprisonment and exile was awarded to loyalty combined with honesty and Liberalism, shown on several occasions by good and esteemed citizens. Our readers had an instance of that kind in the preceding chapter, and will find another in detail, if they read G. Kennan's article "The Last Appeal of the Russian Liberals."

Such was the attitude of Alexander II. and his son and successor has followed his example : tired of having to deal with separate instances of the "breach of discipline" in the *zemstvos*, he has "reformed" them by reducing them to mere tools in the hands of the administration.

We see now the fruit of it. The peaceful elements of society, after having kept for years to the fantastic idea of replacing the present working arbitrary mode of government by a representative one and at the same time remaining loyal to autocracy, came finally to the conclusion that the present autocratic Russian Government would never give up its unnatural prerogatives unless forced to do so by the pressure of popular wishes. We know that the political arrests in Russia carried out this year on a large scale and with precautions which showed that the Government apprehended unusual danger for itself, revealed the existence of a vast organisation, including people of a certain social standing, and of high education, and also of a number of young people studying in universities, acadamies, and other such educational institutions. This organisation calls itself the " Party of Political Right " (Narodnaya Volya) the platform of which as set forth in its secretly printed manifesto is identical with the claims put forward at different times, partly or in full, by the different *zemstvos*, assemblies of nobility, town councils, and the Liberal press. The manifesto runs as follows :—

" *Manifesto of the ' Popular Right ' (Narodnoe Pravo) Party.*

" There are moments in the life of States when one question occupies the foremost place, thrusting into the background all other interests, however essential they may be of themselves—one question, upon the solution of which in one way or another depends the future of the people. Such a moment Russia is now living through, and such a question, determining her further destinies, is the question of political freedom. Autocracy, after receiving its most vivid expression and impersonation in the reign of Alexander III., has with irrefutable clearness proved its impotence to create such an order of things as should secure the country the fullest and most regular developments and all her spiritual and material forces. The tendency of the present reign, expressed with a peculiar sharpness in the reforms (!) of the last few years, in the shape of the institution of rural authorities (Zemskie Nachalniki) and the limitation of the organs of self-government, as also in the systematic support afforded to capitalistic production, clearly shows that the Government continues to pursue inflexibly a policy of administrative arbitrariness and class interests, wholly ignoring the perfectly matured questions of national and social life. The result of this policy has been the social demoralisation and the extreme decline of the country, to avert the consequences and development of which is no longer in the power of the Government. All who recognise the whole danger of the situation see no other issue than an abrupt turn in the direction of the interests of the masses, which is possible only with the immediate participation of the country in the Government—that is, with the replacement of autocracy by free representative institutions.

"As there is not, and cannot be, a hope that the Government will willingly enter upon the path indicated, there is but one course remaining to the people: to oppose the force of organised public opinion to the inertness of the Government and the narrow dynastic interests of the autocracy. The party of Popular Right ('Narodnoe Pravo') has in view the creation of this force.

" In the opinion of the party, popular right includes in itself alike the conception of the right of the people to political freedom and the conception of its right to secure its material needs upon the basis of national production. The party considers the guarantees of this right to be—

" Representative government on the basis of universal suffrage.

" Freedom of religious belief.

" Independence of the courts of justice.

" Freedom of the press.

" Freedom of meeting and association.

" Inviolability of the individual and of his rights as a man.

"In view of the fact that Russia is not a homogeneous whole, but a very complex political body, a necessary condition of political freedom is the recognition of the right to political self-determination, for all the nationalities entering into its composition.

" Thus understanding Popular Right, the party sets itself the task of uniting all the oppositional elements of the country and of organising an active force which should, with all the spiritual and material means at its disposal, attain the overthrow of autocracy and secure to every one the rights of a citizen and a man.

" Being convinced that its aspirations fully correspond to the demands of the historical moment, the party hopes that its call will meet with a warm response in the heads of those who have not yet lost the feeling of human dignity, in whom autocracy has not eaten away the consciousness of their civil rights, who are weary of the yoke of violence and arbitrariness, and to whom are dear the commonweal and the highest ideals of truth and justice."

The " Popular Right " seems to have taken root in every part of the country and in every class of society, the official class included. Therefore the measures taken against it can hardly attain their end, or they have very often to be administered by the secret adherents of the party, and although the state police exult in their recent work, other signs indicate that by making several hundred arrests they have only touched the outskirts of the movement. The Tzar himself and his advisers seem to understand that they can no longer rely on their own bureaucracy. This is shown by the revival of an institution from the time of Nicolas I., a special committee to control all official appointments in the name of the Tzar. Of course it would be childish to imagine that such an institution which might

have had some significance at the time when serfdom existed in all its rigour, when life was simple
and no public opinion existed, could prevent the
development of a political movement at a time when
the population has enormously increased, life become
complicated and public opinion is no longer a myth.
History cannot be stopped, and it is not impossible
that even our generation will see yet great political
changes in Russia.

The Gresham Press,
UNWIN BROTHERS,
CHILWORTH AND LONDON.

Lightning Source UK Ltd.
Milton Keynes UK
UKHW010904070819
347551UK00002B/378/P

9 781408 689431